MBA
12 - Day

Step-by-Step Guide taught

in top business schools for success in job & business

Gyan Shankar

Gyan Shankar

Copyright © Author, Gyan Shankar

2024 Edition

Preface

Ever dreamt of the strategic insights and business acumen gained from a top-tier MBA program, but time or resources have held you back? "MBA 12-Day" offers you a compelling alternative. In this guide, renowned management consultant and educator Gyan Shankar distils the core elements of a prestigious MBA curriculum into a transformative 12-day journey.

Each day, immerse yourself in a critical area of business— from Accounting and Financial Statements to Marketing, Organizational Behaviour, and Strategic Management. This comprehensive guide breaks down complex theories and practical applications, making them accessible and actionable, whether you're a professional seeking to enhance your skills or a student preparing for management roles.

With chapters designed to be both a succinct revision tool and a deep dive into essential MBA concepts, "MBA 12-Day" equips you with the knowledge and mindset to excel in today's competitive business landscape. Unlock the tools and strategies used by top business schools, and elevate your career with confidence and clarity.

Whether you need a quick refresher or a thorough introduction to MBA principles, this book is your gateway to mastering the essentials in just 12 days.

An author with an impressive array of post-graduate degrees and diplomas, including an MBA (West Virginia), brings a wealth of knowledge and practical insights to this essential guide.

Gyan Shankar

Content

Day 1 Accounting   P 7

Day 2 Financial Information & Statement   P 23

Day 3 Marketing   P 30

Day 4 Organisation Behaviour   P 95

Day 5 Entrepreneurship   P 104

Day 6 Strategic Management   P 120

Day 7 Operation Management   P 127

Day 8 Competitive Intelligence   P 135

Day 9 International Business   P 145

Day 10 Negotiation in Business   P 167

Day 11 Organizational Leadership   P 180

Day 12 Advertising   P 200

Gyan Shankar

DAY1

Accounting

The ability to be able to interpret, analyse and use accounting information is critical to the personal success of individuals and the organizations for which they work. Accounting provides quantitative information that enables managers to make informed business decisions. Without a basic understanding of financial statements, accounting methods, and accounting measurement issues, much of the data analysis and interpretation required for business problems would not be possible.

Accounting is the process of recording and analysing transactions that involve events that can be assigned a monetary value. This covers the basic assembly and interpretation of raw financial data, from double-entry bookkeeping through to the construction of the key accounting reports – income statement/profit and loss, cash flow and balance sheet. It continues through to the accounting concepts and ground rules the auditing process and the tools required to assess a business's financial health and performance.

Accounting today is a highly developed field, complete with codified rules, regulatory bodies, and professional certifications that signify degrees of individual expertise. Accounting is often called "the language of business," and for good reason. It provides a structural framework and a quantitative vocabulary with which most business issues and their solutions may be expressed. Managers, investors, and countless others would find themselves virtually paralyzed without the information provided by the accounting process. With such information the foundation can be built for understanding most business issues. The significant demand for relevant, reliable, and timely financial information by capital markets, managers, regulators, and others makes the understanding of the accounting process of critical importance to business.

The accounting discipline is also separated into several sub-disciplines which have different purposes. The main division is into financial accounting and management accounting. MBA Accounting explains how both financial and management accounting are used to assess business performance and to plan, control and make decisions on business activities.

Financial accounting is highly regulated and the information disclosed is expected to be very reliable. It is also the aim of financial accounting to make the information relevant to the external user. Financial accounting is normally concerned with the activities of the entire organization, and for several companies the information will be in the public domain. The intended user of financial statements is external to the organization. Because of the public availability of a company's financial statements, most countries have regulations on the generation and dissemination of these statements. This may be by law, stock exchange regulations and accounting standards. These three forces combined together are known as Generally Accepted Accounting Principles (GAAP), and the most influential and pervasive is accounting standards.

Management accounting is directed towards internal activities and managements' needs for information, which helps them to plan and control activities and to make decisions. It is aimed at providing highly relevant information for managers inside the company. This information should assist them with their responsibilities of planning and controlling the activities of the organization and making decisions. The information is rarely publicly available, and the methods and techniques are developed to meet the requirements of the organization.

An MBA is unlikely to be required to perform the recording side of the accounting process. But it is only by knowing how accounts are prepared and the rules governing the categorizing of assets and liabilities that you can gain a good understanding of what the figures mean. For example, it is not obvious to the uninitiated that a company's shares are classed as a liability and that there is not the remotest possibility that the assets as recorded will realize anything like the figures shown in the accounts.

There is considerable scope for interpretation and educated guesswork as all the facts are rarely available when the accounts are drawn up. For example, we may not know for certain that a particular customer will pay up, yet unless we have firm evidence that they won't, for example, if the business is failing, then the value of the money owed will appear in the accounts. So certain ground rules have been laid down by the profession to help get a level of consistency into accounting information.

The broad dimensions of accounting are the following.

Business Entity

The accounts are kept for the business itself, rather than for the owner(s), bankers, or anyone else associated with the firm. The concept states that assets and liabilities are always defined from the business's viewpoint. So, for example, were a business owner to lend his business money it would appear in the accounts as a liability, though in effect he might see it as his own money. Anything done with that money, say buying equipment, would appear in the accounts as an asset of the business. The owner's stake is accounted for only by the increase or decrease in net.

Money Measurement

In accounting, a record is kept only of the facts that can be expressed in money terms. Expressing business facts in money terms has the great advantage of providing a common denominator. Just imagine trying to add computer equipment and vehicles, together with a 5,000 sq. m office, and then arriving at a total. You need a common term to be able to carry out the basic arithmetical functions and to compare one set of accounts with another, and that term is money.

The things that do not reflect in money terms are excluded. For example, the state of the managing director's health and the news that your main competitor is opening up right opposite in a more attractive outlet are important business facts. However, no accounting record of them is made, however, and they do not show up on the balance sheet, simply because no objective monetary value can be assigned to these facts.

Cost Concept Assets

These are usually entered into the accounts as the cost at the date of purchase. For objectivity, the accountants have settled for cost as the figure to record. It does not mean that the 'cost' figure remains unchanged forever. For example, a motor vehicle costing US $/£/€6,000 may end up looking higher or lower. The period will be determined by factors such as the working life of the asset.

The tax authorities do not allow depreciation as a business expense, so this figure can't be manipulated to reduce tax liability. Other assets, such as freehold land and buildings, will be revalued from time to time, and stock will be entered at cost, or market value, whichever is the lower

Market value is usually used when an asset is actually to be sold and there is an established market for that particular type of asset. Fair value is described as the estimated price at which an asset could be exchanged between knowledgeable but unrelated willing parties who have not, and may not, actually exchange. Market-to-market value is calculated daily, usually by financial institutions such as banks and stockbrokers.

Accounting Reports

Accounting reports always assume that a business will continue trading indefinitely into the future. This means that the assets of the business are looked at simply as profit generators and not as being available for sale. Once a business stops trading, we cannot realistically look at the assets in the same way.

Dual Aspect

To keep a complete record of any business transaction we need to know both where money came from and what has been done with it. It is also possible that some of the products dispatched may be returned at some later date – perhaps for quality reasons. This means that income, and consequently profit, can be brought into the business in one period and has to be removed later on.

Accounting conventions

The accounting professional bodies, with a little prodding from governments, are responsible for ensuring that accounting reports conform to what are known as Generally Accepted Accounting Practices (GAAP).

Although an MBA isn't usually expected to know all the rules, you should be able to get up to date before any meetings where the subject is likely to come up.

Protecting investors

Every country makes rules & regulation protecting investors. For instance, 'The Public Company Accounting Reforms and Investor Protection Act – 2002' of US. The Companies (Audit, Investigations and Community Enterprise) Act of UK.

Auditors

All public companies, that is, those listed on a stock exchange, are required to have an annual audit by a qualified accountant appointed by the directors and approved by the shareholders. The auditors' job is to examine the accounts, ensure that they conform with the prevailing accounting rules and give an opinion about the financial statements.

Cash Flow

There is a saying in business that *profit is vanity and cash flow is sanity.* A cash-flow statement for the year summarizes exactly where cash came from and how it was spent during the year. The cash-flow statement then gives us a complete picture of how cash movements came about: from normal sales activities; the purchase or disposal of assets; or from financing activities. This is an expansion of the sparse single figure in the company's closing balance sheet stating that cash in current assets is £15,751 thousand.

Cash flow is looked at in two distinct and important ways: as a projection of future expected cash flows, and as an analysis of where cash came from and went to in an accounting period and the resultant increase or decrease in cash available.

The future is impossible to predict with great accuracy but it is possible to anticipate likely outcomes and be prepared to deal with events by building in a margin of safety. The starting point of cash-flow forecasts for projecting is to make some assumptions about what you want to achieve and test those for reasonableness.

The income statement and the balance sheet result from accruals and allocations made by accountants, it can be difficult to tell what happened to the firm in terms of the actual flows of cash. Did the firm generate more cash this year than last? The statement of cash flows helps answer this question. It recasts the performance of the firm in cash-based accounting and helps the reader understand the changes in cash and the causes. This statement is also often viewed as supplemental, as it merely specifies in detail how the cash on the balance sheet changes from period to period. It further segregates these changes as those relating to operations, investing, and to financing activities. Contained within each of these statements is a series of accounts, into which the transactions within the firm are recorded. Individual accounts therefore only provide additional detail about the fundamental accounting equation that is expressed in terms of assets, liabilities, and owners' equity, as described earlier.

Balance sheet. This financial report presents a snapshot of the assets of the firm, and the claims upon those assets, at a particular point in time (i.e., the end of the fiscal year). The balance sheet is grounded in the balancing equation summarized earlier and attempts to provide details regarding the firm's assets, liabilities, and owners' equity.

Balance Sheet Equation

The foundation of accounting rests with this fundamental concept. This concept mirrors what should be economic intuition about the firm. Those providing capital investments to the firm (i.e., investors) have claims equivalent to the assets standing behind those investments. In this sense, there must be balance—a balance that can be expressed as assets equal liabilities plus owners' equity. Consider the basic power of this equation. Increases in a firm's assets must be financed by increases in liabilities (e.g., a bank loan) in equity (e.g., a sale of stock), or by creating value through operations. Decreases in assets (such as a debt payment or a dividend payment) must be offset with decreases in that corresponding type of capital (e.g., liabilities or owners' equity, respectively). Changes (or Δ) in an element of the accounting system must likewise be balanced out: Assets = Liabilities + Owners' Equity

To illustrate, consider what happens when the firm borrows capital from a bank. The cash received represents a new asset to the firm, but there is now a new claim against the firm that must be recorded as a liability. So, assets increase by the amount borrowed (i.e., cash), and so do liabilities, and together these changes force a balance of the fundamental accounting equation. As another illustration, consider what happens on the other side of this transaction—that is, from the bank's perspective. The bank has given up cash, but has a new asset that would be labelled as a receivable. The reduction of one asset, cash, is exactly offset by the creation of another, a receivable. From the balance sheet equation and these two examples, one can readily see that even the simplest transaction must have at least two sides, for a minimum of two accounting effects necessary to capture the nature of balancing. Perhaps you have heard of the term double-entry accounting system. The previous balancing equation is the basis for that system.

Income statement.

This financial report is a measure of the flows of business over a period expressed in terms of profit and loss. Profits are expressed in terms of the total revenue activities of the firm, reduced by the costs incurred to generate those revenues. Some of these flows must be adjusted (or matched) across periods to correspond with other flows that are economically related. The activity captured in an income statement is reflected as certain changes on the balance sheet. Because net profit belongs to the owners of the firm, it is in the owners' equity section of the balance sheet that profit will be reported. The individual account capturing profit and loss is commonly referred to as retained earnings.

Accrual Accounting

The notion of reporting over distinct periods is an important feature of financial accounting. Because financial statement users desire to evaluate performance over time, the accounting process must be closed as of a specific date (quarter or year-end), and adjustments to some accounts become necessary. Consider that for all practical purposes, the accounting process follows predictable mechanical cycles each period. This process entails two distinct activities: the everyday recording of transactions during the period, and adjustments of certain key financial statement accounts after the period has ended. For the former, management sets accounting policies and procedures, and chooses accounting methods consistent with required standards—generally accepted accounting principles (GAAP)—that govern how each identifiable event will be recorded. There are choices here, such as whether to depreciate equipment uniformly or use accelerated depreciation, but the decision should be made to accurately reflect the underlying economics of the activity under measurement. For the latter, the accounting cycle is structured such that many estimates and judgments are adjustments made after a reporting period is complete. There are again choices here, such as how long the remaining life is on that same piece of equipment. To appreciate the difference in these two activities, note first that the income statements and balance sheets you will see prepared for public U.S. companies are based on the accrual basis of accounting. Loosely speaking, the underlying tenet of accrual accounting is that assets and liabilities can build and shrink over time, with or without an actual exchange of cash. With these changing assets and liabilities come related changes in the net equity of the corporation (i.e., shareholder wealth). Consider a sale made on customer credit with the payment by that customer expected to occur sometime next year. This first activity is a day-to-day transaction that would increase the earnings and asset base of the firm. If the customer's account is still outstanding at the end of the quarter when the books must be closed, the second activity, an adjustment, may take place. Specifically, an adjustment for this account may be necessary for an estimated amount the manager believes will be uncollectible. For this credit sale event, also note that accrual accounting would dictate that there have been earnings this year, but none next. How? An asset, accounts receivable, will be recorded that reflects an increase in the net earnings of the firm (top-line revenue). Why this year and not next? Because it was this year that the fruits of the firm's effort have been realized. As long as it is reasonably certain that payment will be made, the customer's financing decision should have little to do with communicating to outsiders how well the firm did this year, and likewise what the existing asset base should be. Most entities of any complexity use the accrual basis of accounting, which recognizes the financial effect of an activity when the activity takes place, without regard to the timing of its cash effects. For its part, the accrual accounting process depends on various allocation and matching decisions. Consider that measuring financial success would be simple if an entity had only to summarize and report its activities at the end of its life. Cash results and accrual results would be exactly the same: We would measure results by simply asking whether the owners of the company had more cash at the end than they had at the start. However, both management and outsiders demand information about an entity's performance during interim periods of its life. Accounting rules and conventions are designed to allocate (or assign) the financial effect of an entity's activities to specific periods. Accounting standards and conventions are also designed to comprehensively report all of a transaction's financial effects in the applicable period. The objective of this matching principle is to report revenues in the period in which they are earned and to report all.

A Step-by-Step Guide to Reading Annual Reports

Reading financial statements is one of the best ways to gain an understanding of accounting and its significance to business. The annual report, however, is more than simply a means by which to provide accounting data. Companies often will use this document to communicate their organizational stories, both documenting the company's historical evolution and outlining future strategic plans. The following seven recommended steps illustrate one way to approach getting the most out of reading the typical annual report.

Step 1: Pay attention to the themes in the opening letter to shareholders. The letter to shareholders is usually the first item in the annual report and is valuable on many dimensions, but mainly for understanding at the start the strategic intent of the managers of the firm. The letter usually sums up performance during the past year and expresses elements of the CEO's goals, values, and vision for the future. As an example, the letter in the 2008 Annual Report from Indra K. Nooyi, Chairman and CEO of PepsiCo, references the new strategic mission rolled out two years earlier, discusses how the company is delivering on objectives while navigating through the current recession, and highlights certain financial trends of importance to shareholders. The letter conveys a sense of practicality while emphasizing to shareholders that the company prevailed during tough times because "our teams of extraordinary people applied their can-do spirit and must-do sense of responsibility to meet the economic and market challenges head-on."

Step 2: Check the Auditor's Letter

Investors in companies ordinarily require an annual audit of those companies' financial statements. As described earlier for publicly traded companies, this is mandatory. The independent annual audit is one of the most basic protections intended to ensure compliance with GAAP. At the end of the financial report, one will find a letter from the firm's independent auditors that explains what they did and what they concluded. The astute reader of an annual report will always check the audit report, because anything but a positive report should, like a flashing red light, signal a major concern worth further investigation.

Step 3: Review the Income Statement

The income statement is prepared using accrual accounting and summarizes the operating performance of the firm. It is organized on the principle that what customers buy (e.g., revenues), less what it costs to enable them to buy (e.g., expenses), results in profits. Recognizing this basic notion can help the reader sort out three concerns in looking at the income statement:

1. The degree of profitability, and why. Is the company making or losing money?

2. The trend of profitability, and why. Are profits increasing or declining over time? Are these due to changes in revenues, expenses, or both?

3. The composition of profits. Are the size and trend of profits due to ordinary operations, or to odd events that might distort the true profitability of the firm?

Step 4: Review the Balance Sheet

For most balance sheets, the major categories of assets are classified and ranked according to their liquidity, with cash, short-term investments, and other current assets (those that should be converted to cash within one year) at the top, and less liquid assets at the bottom. For the remainder of the statement, current liabilities (those due within one year) are listed first. Next comes debt and other liabilities, and toward the bottom is shareholders' equity, the residual claim on the firm.

Many are not reported. In reading the balance sheet, one should aim to satisfy four questions:

1. Is the firm solvent? Solvency is the ability to pay liabilities as they come due. The back-of-the-envelope test of this is to first observe by how much the value of assets exceeds the value of liabilities.

2. Are the firm's assets sufficiently liquid? Liquidity measures the ability to meet near-term cash obligations—these might be liabilities that need to be repaid, or they might be a forthcoming payroll or the need to purchase raw materials in advance of a sudden surge in demand.

3. What is the mix of assets? The reader should look for unusual concentrations or categories of assets. Concentration of the firm's resources into a speculative venture would be a cause for concern. Concentration in cash might suggest undue risk aversion or the lack of investment opportunities with attractive return potential. Also, asset categories that seem to have no relevance to the firm's business purpose should raise a red flag.

4. What is the mix of financing? Most mature firms finance their businesses with some debt. The absence of debt or a very high proportion of debt should raise questions about the outlook of senior management, and/or the bets they are making. Again, odd categories of capital (e.g., exchangeable subordinated bonds) may indicate managerial creativity, or they may indicate desperation on the part of management—either way, they should invite the thoughtful reader of the annual report to dig deeper.

Step 5: Review the Statement of Cash Flows

The statement of cash flows reports the cash receipts and outflows classified as operating, investing, and financing activities—this breakdown helps the reader determine where changes in cash emerge. The key questions a reader should ask include:

• Was the firm a net user or generator of cash for the year?
• What operational, investing, or financing elements proved to be major drivers of cash flow?
• Are there any major departures in the trends of the cash flow items?

Step 6: Read the Footnotes to the Financial Statements

A set of footnotes immediately follows the financial statements, typically spans many pages, and is considered by regulators to be an integral part of the financial statements. The footnotes tend to amplify and clarify information not readily apparent from reference to the statements themselves. For instance, the footnotes to PepsiCo's report offer, among others, the following important information:

Footnotes can be very technical and difficult for the novice to understand. But most users of annual reports would tell that they contain many important insights about a company not found elsewhere. At a minimum, footnotes should be referenced as necessary when questions arise in your review of the financial statements.

Step-7. Assessing the financial health of the firm:

Financial ratios show the performance of the firm in four important areas:

1. Profitability is measured both in terms of profit or expense margins and as investment return. Investors typically will focus on return on assets, return on equity, and profit margin.

2. Leverage ratios measure the use of short-term and long-term debt financing by the firm. In general, higher usage of debt increases the risk of the firm and is of particular concern during times of economic recession. Higher ratios of debt to total capital invested suggest a company seeking higher net returns, but one also willing to take on higher financial risk. The ratio of times interest earned measures the ability of the firm to cover its interest payments; lower levels of this ratio suggest high risk and poor relative operating performance.

3. Asset efficiency and utilization ratios measure how well the firm deploys its assets.

The asset turnover ratio (sales over assets) indicates how many dollars of sales are generated per dollar of assets in use; a higher figure suggests more efficiency.

Liquidity ratios measure the resources available to meet short-term financial commitments, should that be required. The current ratio answers the question of whether the company has enough current assets to cover all current liabilities.

However, it can be difficult to assemble a unified view of the firm from these ratios. Fortunately, the DuPont system of ratios can help analysts integrate their insights. The DuPont system was developed during World War I when the financial officers of E.I. du Pont de Nemours and Company sought a system to assess the health of their firm and of the segments within the firm. This system decomposes return on equity into several constituent pieces: profit margin, which measures the profitability of each dollar of revenue; sales turnover, which measures the dollars of sales produced by each dollar of assets; and the ratio of assets to equity, which measures the financial leverage of the company, or the dollars of assets carried by each dollar of equity.

DAY 2

Financial Information & Statement

Business finance comprises several disciplinary areas, each with several components. The disciplines contain the tools with which you can effectively analyse a business's financial situation, drawing on both internal information relevant to the business and external information on its markets, competitors and general business environment as a prelude to deciding what to do.

The ultimate success of the product the carpenter makes is partly down to his or her skills in using those tools and partly down to the world he or she is operating in at a particular time. In business, for example, there is no such thing as an optimal capital structure, or the right number of new products to bring to market, or whether or not going for an acquisition is a winning strategy.

Financial statements are like the tip of an iceberg, underneath the visible part are a lot of record-keeping, accounting methods and reporting decisions. The managers of a business, the investors in a business and the lenders to a business need a firm grasp on these accounting reports so they will know how to recognize both the good and bad signals.

Financial statements contain critically important business information and are used for many different purposes by many different parties inside the business and outside of the business. All successful businesspeople should have a good basic understanding of financial statements and the main financial ratios, such as profit margin, asset turnover, return on assets, and return on equity.

Accountants prepare three primary financial statements. The profit and loss account (income statement in the United States) reports the profit-making activities of the business and how much profit or loss the business made. The balance sheet reports the financial situation and position of the business in terms of its assets and liabilities at a point in time and usually the last day of the profit period. The cash flow statement reports how much cash was realized from profit and other sources of cash, and what the business did with this money. In short, the financial life of a business and its prospects for success or danger of failing are all revealed in its financial statements.

Who uses financial information and why?

All accounting information aims to provide the particular user with relevant and timely data to make decisions. Possible users are an extensive group, who require the information to be impartial, accurate and timely.

Following group of use financial information of the company:

- The shareholders of limited companies will be influenced in their decision to remain investors or to increase/decrease their holding by receiving information about the financial performance and financial position of the company. This usually occurs twice a year in the form of a profit and loss account and a balance sheet relating to the first half-year and, later on, the full year.
- Existing equity investors and lenders, to monitor their investments and evaluate the performance of management.
- Prospective equity investors and lenders, to decide whether to invest.
- Investment analysts, money managers, and stockbrokers to make buy/sell/hold recommendations to their clients.
- Rating agencies (such as Moody's Investors Service, Standard & Poor's, and Fitch Ratings), to assign credit ratings, or Dun & Bradstreet, to obtain business information reports.5. Major customers and suppliers, to evaluate the financial strength and staying power of the company as a dependable resource for their business.
- Owner-managers of non-incorporated businesses will require the above information but they will also be privy to more detailed and more frequent

information about the business's financial affairs. Management in companies ranges from director level down to supervisor level. Each person requires accounting information to help him or her in his or her role.

- The board of directors, to review the performance of management.
- Management, to assess its performance
- Suppliers need to assess the creditworthiness of potential and existing customers when setting the amount and period of credit allowed. Customers also need to be reassured, in this case, to minimize the risk of their supplies drying up and disrupting their output.
- Employees and their representatives have a vested interest in the financial health and prospects of their employer.
- Labour unions, to gauge how much of a pay increase a company can afford in upcoming labour negotiations
- Corporate raiders, to seek hidden value in companies with under-priced stock.
- Competitors, to benchmark their financial results.
- Potential competitors, to assess how profitable it may be to enter an industry.
- Government agencies responsible for taxing, regulating, or investigating the company.
- Politicians, lobbyists, issue groups, consumer advocates, environmentalists, think tanks,

foundations, media reporters, and others who support or oppose any particular issue.

• Actual or potential joint venture partners, franchisors or franchisees, and other business interests that have a reason to be informed about the company and its financial situation.

Basic Points in Financial Statements

1. The basic form of the balance sheet is Assets = Liabilities + Owner Equity.

2. Assets are expenditures made for items such as inventory and equipment that are needed to operate the business. The liabilities and owner equity reflect the funds that financed the expenditures for the assets.

3. Balance sheets show the financial position of a business at a given moment.

4. Balance sheets change as transactions are recorded.

5. Every transaction is an exchange, and both sides of each transaction are recorded. For example, when a bank loan is made, there is an increase in cash, which is matched by an increase in a liability entitled "Bank loan." When a bank loan is repaid, there is a decrease in cash, which is matched by a decrease in a liability entitled "Bank loan." After every transaction, the balance sheet stays in balance.

6. Income increases owner equity, and drawings decrease owner equity.

7. The income statement shows how the income for the period was earned.

8. The basic form of the income statement:

  a. Sales - Cost of Goods Sold = Gross Income.

  b. Gross Income - Expenses = Net Income.

9. The income statement is simply a detailed explanation of the increase in owner equity represented by net income. It shows how the owner equity increased from the beginning of the year to the end of the year on account of the net income.

10. Net income contributes to cash from operations, after it has been adjusted to a cash basis.

11. Not all expenses are cash outflows: for instance, depreciation.

12. Changes in current assets (except cash) and current liabilities are not cash outflows or inflows, respectively, in the period under consideration. They represent future, rather than present, cash flows.

13. Cash can be generated internally by operations, or externally from outside sources such as lenders (or equity investors).

14. The cash flow statement is simply a detailed explanation of how cash at the start developed into cash at the end by cash inflows, generated internally and externally, less cash outflows.

15. The income statement is an elaboration of the change in owner equity in the balance sheet caused by earning income.

The cash flow statement is an elaboration of the balance sheet change in beginning and ending cash. Therefore, all three financial statements are interrelated, or, to use the technical term, "articulated." They are mutually consistent, and that is why they are referred to as a "set" of financial statements. The three-piece set consists of a balance sheet, income statement, and cash flow statement.

16. A set of financial statements can convey valuable information about the enterprise to anyone who knows how to analyse financial statements. This information goes to the core of the organization's business strategy and the effectiveness of its management.

DAY 3

Marketing

Marketing is defined as the process that ensures the right products and services get to the right markets at the right time and at the right price. The key word in that sentence is the word 'right'. The deal has to work for the customer because if they don't want what you have to offer the game is over before you begin. You have to offer value and satisfaction, otherwise, people will either choose a superior competitor or, if they do buy from you and are dissatisfied, they won't buy again.

For you, the marketer, being right means there have to be enough people wanting your product or service to make the venture profitable; and ideally, those numbers should be getting bigger rather than smaller.

The boundaries of marketing stretch back from inside the mind of the customer, perhaps uncovering emotions he or she was barely aware of, out to the logistic support systems that get the product or service into the customer's hands. Each part of the value chain from company to consumer has the potential to add value or kill the deal.

All products and services have markets that comprise consumers. However, there are two fundamentally different types of markets. The first is consumer markets where the product or service is largely bought and used by the same person, or someone close to them, for personal satisfaction rather than financial gain. The second is business-to-business (B2B) markets where both parties to the transaction expect to make money and both may simply be in the chain that links to end-consumers. A food processing company making pizzas would buy ingredients from other businesses and sell to outlets such as supermarkets or other retailers. They in turn would sell to someone who eats the pizza. It could of course be that they merely bought the product for some other family member to consume. Markets can be complicated, messy affairs and the marketer has to get an understanding of all the forces at work along the path from materials to end consumption or use.

Consumers

The same product or service can be used for a variety of purposes, by different end-consumers to gain quite different satisfactions or to meet quite different needs. Marketing to consumers requires getting under their skin to see what their needs, desires, preferences and aspirations are: all the subjects of later chapters. Also, of course, where they will buy – online or offline – and how much they are prepared to pay, factors that are influenced by their socioeconomic and educational background, amongst other factors. The problem for the marketer is that markets don't stand still and the most profitable path may move from selling B2B to end-consumers as markets mature and develop.

Business-to-business markets

Although invisible to the end consumer, the B2B market is bigger, more diverse, complex and profitable than the consumer market. To return to our pizza buyer, before that is available in the retail outlet dozens of businesses have played their part in the process. The cheese topping alone, just one of several ingredients that are assembled in the final pizza product, goes through many business hands before it gets to the retailer. Take milk, for example. Cows have to be bred, fed, kept healthy and warm, milked efficiently and that milk distributed from dairy to units for further processing. These business-to-business transactions involve farmers, fertilizer companies, milking equipment manufacturers, builders, transporters and cheese processors, amongst others.

The most credible claim for being the internet's midwife probably goes to Tim Berners-Lee, a consultant working for CERN, the European Organization for Nuclear Research. In June–December of 1980 he wrote a notebook program, 'Enquire-within-upon-everything', that allowed links to be made between arbitrary nodes. Each node had a title, a type and a list of bidirectional typed links. 'Enquire' ran on Norsk Data machines under SINTRAN-III. Berners-Lee's goal was to allow the different computer systems used by the experts assembled from dozens to countries to 'talk' to each other both within CERN itself and with colleagues around the globe. In August 2022 around 70 per cent of the world's close to 8 billion population had access to the internet. In North America and Europe, that proportion was above 90 per cent.

Richness vs reach

The internet has largely changed the maths of the traditional trade-off between the economics of delivering individually tailored products and services to satisfy targeted customers and the requirement of businesses to achieve economies of scale. The near-impossible second-hand book that had to be tracked down laboriously and at some cost is now just a mouse click away. The cost of keeping a retail operation open all hours is untenable but sales can continue online all the time. A small business that once couldn't have considered going global until many years into its life can today, thanks to the internet.

The internet has made real what in the 1970s Marshall McLuhan, a Canadian visionary of marketing communications, called the 'global village'. A United Nations report, How COVID-19 Triggered the Digital and E-commerce Turning Point, published in March 2021, observed, 'we will look back at 2020 as the moment that changed everything. Nowhere else has unprecedented and unforeseen growth occurred as in the digital and e-commerce sectors, which have boomed amid the Covid-19 crisis.'

Marketers have always had an appetite for data. However, the internet has added two important twists to information gathering. In the first instance, the information can be assembled in real-time. That means the information is current and so probably more valid than that gleaned weeks or months ago when different circumstances might have prevailed. Breaking down barriers and levelling the playing field.

One of the criteria for a successful marketing strategy is to ensure that new entrants can't enter the market easily or at least without at least as much cost as you have incurred. The internet era has levelled the playing field between big established businesses and new market entrants.

Clicks and bricks

Of course, the internet business world and the 'real' world overlap and, in some cases, take over from one another. Woolworths, for example, died on the high street in 2009 only to be born again on the internet.

Viral marketing

This term was coined to describe the ability of the internet to accelerate interest and awareness in a product by rapid word-of-mouth communications.

A new world – new threats.

Even if firms think that e-business offers few advantages, they could find themselves facing a range of new threats. For example, the competitors that offline businesses face are small and big firms in their own country or area and international firms from elsewhere in the world. With the internet, they could now have small firms similar to themselves but based anywhere in the world, entering their market. Potentially this could put them up against hundreds of new competitors. New world – old opportunities. Of course, the internet has not replaced old-world maxims and opportunities.

Buying Process

Before making a purchase, people go through several different stages unique to each purchase. Businesses often try to figure out these stages to help customers better and improve their reputation and sales as a whole.

Before a consumer buy anything, they will go through a series of steps. If marketers and business owners can understand these steps and what the consumer is thinking during each one, they can tailor their marketing to influence a consumer's purchasing decision and promote customer retention.

The steps a consumer commonly takes when making a buying decision is known in marketing as the buying process. The customer buying process refers to the steps that a customer takes when making a purchase decision. It is a journey that begins when a customer recognizes a need or desire and ends when the customer is satisfied with the product or service purchased. Importance of customer buying process

The customer buying process is important for businesses because it shows them the steps a customer takes before and after making a purchase.

Importance of customer buying process

The buying process can improve the overall customer experience and make customers more likely to buy from you again and tell their friends about you.

Understanding the customer buying process can also help a business find the best ways to reach customers, make better decisions about product development, and even improve customer service.

The customer purchasing process can also assist businesses in identifying any blockages or obstacles that may be preventing a sale and taking appropriate action to address them.
Understanding the customer purchasing process can assist businesses in increasing sales and improving customer satisfaction.

And finally, understanding the customer purchasing process is important for any company that wants to stay competitive and grow.

The buying Process includes the following six stages. By considering each stage of the consumer buying process (the consumer purchase decision process), you can implement smart strategies for your business at each point along the way — building trust and keeping shoppers engaged at every step. Pick a product of your choice to take through the questions below associated with the five stages of the buying process. Be specific about the exact product you choose. The following are a few examples of product lines you may choose a product from: New Vehicle, Hair Shampoo, Mattress, or Cookies

Stage One: Needs and Wants. Problem recognition

    Identify the needs of the target consumer.
    Identify the wants of the target consumer.
    How did you differentiate between the needs and wants?

Problem recognition is often seen as the first and most important step in the customer buying process. It is impossible to make a purchase without identifying a problem or need. The need may have been caused by something inside or outside of the person, like hunger or thirst (such as advertising or word of mouth).

Customers rarely purchase products and services just for the sake of buying them; they purchase things because it solves a problem and help them reach what they want to achieve.

Essentially, a potential customer will conduct their very own problem identification analysis. For example, if a person feels like he or she needs a new car, that person may be recognizing a need for transportation or adventure. If the desire or requirement for transportation or adventure is strong enough, a consumer will venture into the next stage of the decision-making process—information search.

Make consumers aware that there is a problem worth solving, then present your company and its services as an "ideal solution."

At this stage, building brand awareness is key. You want your target market to already know and trust your business. Especially in today's world where consumers don't just want to shop, they want to support businesses that reflect their values and beliefs.

So much so, that 82% of shoppers say they'd avoid using a brand again if they lost trust.

Stage Two: Information Search

What mediums will you use to ensure the target consumer can find your product?
Does your product have multiple target consumers? If so, does this require multiple mediums for the information search?

After identifying a problem or need, a customer may proceed to the information search stage to determine what they believe is the best solution.

Once a customer recognizes their problem, the search for a suitable solution begins. They know there is an issue and are looking for someone or something to help them fix it. To reach them at this stage, focus on creating valuable information that the potential customer can use to make an informed decision about the products or services you offer. Let customers know you offer services they haven't considered before and appeal to people who may search independently. As a marketer or business owner, this is your best opportunity to establish your brand as an industry leader or expert in the field.

The buyer searches the internal and external business environments to find and evaluate information sources related to the main buying decision. Your customer may get information from written, visual, online, or word-of-mouth sources. As an example of the information search stage, a consumer can search for information by researching different options, talking to friends or family members, or reading reviews online. This stage allows the individual to make a more informed decision about the next stage.

Once consumers are aware they have a want, they're now ready to find out how to fulfil it. And so, their search begins, predominantly on search engines or social media.

In this stage in the consumer buying process, it's imperative to optimize your brand or retail site for search engine optimization (SEO), so you show up in search results. And given that 70% of shoppers use Instagram for product discovery, you'll want to focus on your Instagram SEO too.

How consumers search and what information they'll need is based on how much they already know, and what details they find from fellow shoppers. Commerce today is always-on and consumer-to-consumer-orientated, where consumers are your best salespeople. That's why most brands and retailers turn to user-generated content (UGC), which is any content (reviews, images, Q&As) created by unpaid individuals rather than a brand.

Customer ratings and reviews get your brand seen and help usher people to your site through keyword-rich and relevant content. Search engines reward sites that talk in the same language as customers. So, when your shoppers are the ones creating the content, your brand is more likely to pop up first in the search. UGC is also a way to authentically build trust (there's that T word again) with shoppers, as 79% of consumers say online reviews have as much of an impact as recommendations from friends or family.

Stage Three: Evaluation of Choices. Evaluation of alternatives.

What is the range of choices for consumers in this product sector? How will you influence the decision of your target consumer?

At this stage of the consumer decision process, the consumer will probably know which product will solve their problem, but before committing, they'll compare their potential product or service of choice against alternatives. This is normally done by evaluating it against alternatives based on quality, price, popularity, and reviews.

Individuals will evaluate different products at this stage based on alternative product attributes. The customer's attitude is a major factor in this stage. Another factor influencing the evaluation process is involvement.

For example, if customers' attitudes and involvement are positive, they will evaluate several companies or brands. If it is negative, only one company or brand will be evaluated. The consumer will consider factors such as the costs and benefits of each option as well as how each option aligns with their values and goals. This stage is important because it allows the decision-maker to make an informed choice about the next stage.

Stage Four: Purchasing Decision

How will consumers purchase this product? Will it be online, in-store, an alternative source, or a combination?
What other requirements do you have during the purchase phase specific to your product?

The fourth stage of the decision-making process is the purchasing stage. This is when the consumer decides which product or service to buy.

If all goes to plan and your marketing efforts pay off, the consumer makes their final decision and purchases the product or service. The purchasing decision occurs midway through the five customer buying stages. The customer has considered several options, understands cost and payment, and is determining whether to purchase. Yes, they could still decide to leave at this point.

At this point, customers need a sense of safety. They also needed to be reminded of the problem that had brought them here in the first place. And if a customer decides to leave, this is the best time to get them to come back. Depending on your business, this could be something as simple as an email saying,
"Hey, you were interested in our fashion design!". The customer has already decided to buy from you, so you have to make the process easy for them. If your software for

processing payments is slow, they might leave and go to a competitor.

At this point, shoppers are making a list and checking it twice. They're aware of your brand, have been brought to your site, and are now evaluating whether to purchase from you or a competitor. It's crunch time, and they want to make the best choice. No regrets.

So, what can you do to build confidence that you have what they want? The answer again is UGC. Ratings, reviews, Q&As, and customer photos are what consumers are turning to first to make buying decisions, and they inspire them at every step of the path to purchase. 53% of consumers say UGC makes them more confident in purchase decisions, according to our survey of over 7,000 global shoppers. The need for authenticity is only getting stronger. This trend is expected to flip the future of product display pages with content and opinions from real consumers already replacing professional product information.

Specifically, the factors that affect the purchasing decision include:

Need for the product
Perceived benefits of the product
Perceived risks of the product
Ability to pay for the product
Any social influences that may affect the consumer's decision

Completing the purchase

According to a study by the Baynard Institute, nearly 70% of shopping carts in the e-commerce industry were abandoned before checkout. This comes alongside an increase in analysis paralysis brought on by COVID-19.

Simple decisions feel heavy now. Deciding what to order for dinner can feel as stressful as switching careers.

It's up to you to alleviate this stress by making the purchase decision as simple as possible for consumers. Areas of opportunity for brands and retailers here include:

List total prices upfront so there aren't any surprises
Create an option for guest checkout to give shoppers an alternative to creating a personal account
Keeping checkout lines short
Showcase positive testimonials from reviews on the checkout page to build reassurance
Offer quick commerce services to save shoppers the hassle of in-store pickups

Stage Six: Post-Decision Evaluation.
          Post-purchase evaluation

Does your product possibly require a warranty, replacement, or repair after purchase? If so, how will you provide these services?
What sources of feedback can you implement to improve future marketing?

This is the last stage of the customer buying process, buyers compare things to their expectations and are either satisfied or dissatisfied. As a result, these stages are important for customer retention. It can impact the information search and alternative evaluation stages for future purchases from the same company. Satisfied customers will be loyal to your brand, skipping the Information search and evaluation of alternatives stages.

After purchasing the product, the customer weighs up their purchase and compares it to their overall expectations. This either leads to satisfaction or dissatisfaction.

Customers often leave product reviews based on their satisfaction. Companies should carefully craft good post-purchase communication to engage customers and maximize efficiency. Website, social media, and word-of-mouth reviews are examples.

When a customer is satisfied with a purchase, their actions typically reflect this satisfaction. They may:

Choose to return to the business for future transactions

Recommend the company to friends or family

Provide positive feedback

Conversely, when a customer is dissatisfied, they may take the following actions:
Voicing their complaints to the company
Sharing their frustrations with others
Refusing to do business with the company in the future
Write negative reviews or spread rumours about the company

The product has been purchased. The consumer buying process is complete. But there's still one more step. You now have the unique opportunity to turn the buyer into a repeat customer by keeping them engaged with your brand or store. After all, customer retention is easier and cheaper than new custom.

Asking your customers for feedback on their purchases or using consumer insights found in product reviews is one of the best ways to build brand loyalty. It shows you care about their opinions and the overall experience they had with your business. Retail giants collect UGC to encourage future buyers in their purchase decisions. The brand consistently analyses customer feedback for areas of improvement to increase in conversion rate. Customers are sharper than ever. And they look to their peers for unbiased opinions when making purchasing decisions — an impressive 78% of shoppers globally trust online reviews.

Market Segmentation

By understanding your market segments, you can leverage this targeting in product, sales, and marketing strategies. Market segments can power your product development cycles by informing how you create product offerings for different segments like men vs. women or high income vs. low income.

Business people that understand market segments can prove themselves to be effective marketers while earning a greater return on their investments. Market segments are known to respond somewhat predictably to a marketing strategy, plan, or promotion. This is why marketers use segmentation when deciding on a target market. As its name suggests, market segmentation is the process of separating a market into sub-groups, in which its members share common characteristics.

Market segmentation is a marketing strategy that uses well-defined criteria to divide their product, brand or services complete addressable market share into smaller groups. Each group, or segment, shares common characteristics that enable the brand to create focused and targeted products, offers and experiences. It is a category of customers who have similar likes and dislikes in an otherwise homogeneous market. These customers can be individuals, families, businesses, organizations, or a blend of multiple types

Salient Features of Market Segmentation

1.A market segment is a group of people who share one or more similar characteristics.
2.Corporations and marketing teams use various criteria to develop target markets for their products and services.

3. The criteria for a market segment include homogeneity among the segment's main needs, uniqueness, and a common reaction to marketing tactics.
4. The reaction from market segments to marketing plans or strategies is typically very predictable.
5. Common market segment traits include interests, lifestyle, age, and gender.
6. There must be homogeneity among the common needs of the segment.
7. There needs to be a distinction that makes the segment unique from other groups.
8. The presence of a common reaction or a similar and somewhat predictable response to marketing is required

Market segmentation can be a competitive differentiator. Customers served by market segmentation campaigns may perceive that a brand's messaging and products were specifically tailored to them. A brand's total addressable market can have a variety of needs, challenges, preferences and buying criteria. Market segmentation carves out focused portions of a target market in order to create messaging, products and services that are customized to those segments.

Why is market segmentation important?

Market segmentation results in more effective and efficient marketing, advertising and sales. Rather than targeting a broad audience with generic messaging and offers, market segmentation enables brands to provide offers specifically tailored to each segment's needs. Consider an advertising campaign organized around a particular market segment. A brand can select relevant targeting criteria to reach users who fit the criteria of that market segment.

Market segmentation can result in a campaign that is both effective and efficient: Audience segmenting and customized messaging drives higher success rates, while advertising dollars are only spent to reach the defined audience. The same non-segmented campaign would suffer from lower response rates, with a portion of the advertising budget wasted on the wrong audience.

Commonly used in marketing strategies, market segments help companies optimize their products and services to suit the needs of a given segment. Market segments are often used to identify a target market. Companies who properly segment their market enjoy significant advantages. According to a study by Bain & Company, 81% of executives found that segmentation was crucial for growing profits. Bain also found that organisations with great market segmentation strategies enjoyed a 10% higher profit than companies whose segmentation wasn't as effective over a 5-year period. Companies like American Express, Mercedes Benz, and Best Buy have all used segmentation strategies to increase sales, build better products, and engage better with their prospects and customers.

Other benefits of segmentation include the followings:

Stronger marketing messages: You no longer have to be generic and vague – you can speak directly to a specific group of people in ways they can relate to, because you understand their characteristics, wants, and needs.

Targeted digital advertising: Market segmentation helps you understand and define your audience's characteristics, so you can direct your marketing efforts to specific ages, locations, buying habits, interests etc.

Developing effective marketing strategies: Knowing your target audience gives you a head start about what methods, tactics and solutions they will be most responsive to. better response rates and lower acquisition costs: These will result from creating your marketing communications both in ad messaging and advanced targeting on digital platforms like Facebook and Google using your segmentation.

Attracting the right customers: Market segmentation helps you create targeted, clear and direct messaging that attracts the people you want to buy from you.

Increasing brand loyalty: when customers feel understood, uniquely well-served and trusting, they are more likely to stick with your brand.

Differentiating your brand from the competition: More specific, personal messaging makes your brand stand out.

Identifying niche markets: segmentation can uncover not only underserved markets but also new ways of serving existing markets – opportunities which can be used to grow your brand.

Staying on message: As segmentation is so linear, it's easy to stay on track with your marketing strategies, and not get distracted into less effective areas.

Driving growth: You can encourage customers to buy from you again, or trade up from a lower-priced product or service.

Enhanced profits: Different customers have different disposable incomes; prices can be set according to how much they are willing to spend. Knowing this can ensure you don't over (or under) sell yourself.

Product development: You'll be able to design with the needs of your customers top of mind, and develop different products that cater to your different customer base areas.

Examples of Market Segments

1. Consider a company that markets health and beauty products to both men and women. These products, such as razors or skin care, are typically more expensive for women than they are for men. The product packaging also differs—products targeted to women have pink and floral accents that align with gender stereotypes. On the other hand, the company's male-targeted products are characterized by more rugged blacks and greys.

2. The banking industry provides a very good example of how a company markets to specific market segments. All commercial banks service a wide range of people, many of whom have relatable life situations and monetary goals. If a bank wants to market to baby boomers, it conducts research and may find that retirement planning is the most important aspect of their financial needs. The bank can then market tax-deferred accounts to this consumer segment.

If the same bank wants to effectively market products and services to millennials, say, Roth IRAs and 401(k)s may not be the best option. Instead, the bank may conduct in-depth market research and discover most millennials are planning to have a family. The bank uses that data to market college-friendly savings and investment accounts to this consumer segment.

3. Sometimes a company already has a product but may not yet have its target consumer segment. In this scenario, it is up to the business to define its market and cater its offering to its target group. Restaurants are a good example. If a restaurant is near a college, it can market its

food in such a way as to entice college students to enjoy happy hour rather than trying to attract high-value business customers

Types of Market Segmentation

With segmentation and targeting, you want to understand how your market will respond in a given situation, like purchasing your products. In many cases, a predictive model may be incorporated into the study so that you can group individuals within identified segments based on specific answers to survey questions.

There are four primary types of market segmentation, which include the following:

Demographic segmentation

Demographic segmentation sorts a market by elements such as age, education, income, family size, race, gender, occupation, and nationality. Demographics is one of the simplest and most commonly used forms of segmentation because the products and services we buy, how we use those products, and how much we are willing to spend on them is most often based on demographic factors.

Geographic segmentation is relatively simple to manage, assuming the brand has the location and address information of potential customers. Geographic segmentation works by grouping potential customers by the areas in which they live or reside.

Example geographic market segments include the following:

North America
Europe, Middle East, Africa (EMEA)
Midwest United States
Northeast United States

New York, New Jersey and Connecticut
Northern California and Southern California
Cuyahoga County, Ohio

For geographic market segments, a brand may choose to offer products and services tailored to the following:

Local or regional preferences, such as seasonal offerings like beach and ski season;
Regional tastes like barbecue in the Southern or Midwestern United States; or
Local laws and regulations.

Geographic segmentation

Geographic segmentation can be a subset of demographic segmentation, although it can also be a type of segmentation in its own right. It creates different target customer groups based on geographical boundaries. Because potential customers have needs, preferences, and interests that differ according to their geographies, understanding the climates and geographic regions of customer groups can help determine where to sell and advertise, as well as where to expand your business.

Demographic segmentation

It is also relatively simple to manage, assuming the brand has the necessary demographic information of potential customers. Demographic segmentation works by grouping potential customers by their attributes, such as age, ethnicity, education, job title, industry, marital status and income. A brand may define a demographic market segment based on a single attribute or a combination of several.
Examples of demographic market segments include the following:
Single men;

Married couples with two or more children;
Women with an annual income above $65,000;
Women with a master's degree or related graduate degree;
Men with senior job titles in the automobile industry.

Firmographic Segmentation

Firmographic Segmentation is similar to demographic segmentation, except that demographics look at individuals while firmographics look at organisations. Firmographic segmentation would consider things like company size, and number of employees and would illustrate how addressing a small business would differ from addressing an enterprise corporation.

Behavioural Segmentation

Behavioural Segmentation divides markets by behaviours and decision-making patterns such as purchase, consumption, lifestyle, and usage. For instance, younger buyers may tend to purchase bottled body wash, while older consumer groups may lean towards soap bars. Segmenting markets based on purchase behaviours enables marketers to develop a more targeted approach because you can focus on what you know they, are and are therefore more likely to buy.

Behavioural segmentation is more complex to manage because it requires brands to have access to behavioural data. It also requires the necessary tools to manage that data and create market segments based on it. Behavioural segmentation works by grouping potential customers based on observed actions or behaviours. Actions can include past purchases, lifestyle choices, travel destinations and daily routines. Behavioural data can be observed or queried via online interactions, such as social media posts, forum posts and published reviews.

Examples of behavioural market segments include the following:

  People who purchased a new home in the past 12 months;
  People who take more than 10 flights per year;
  People who drive their kids to sports practices multiple times per week; and
  People who had more than $1,000 in online purchases in the past year.

Psychographic segmentation

Psychographic segmentation considers the psychological aspects of consumer behaviour by dividing markets according to the lifestyle, personality traits, values, opinions, and interests of consumers. Large markets like the fitness market use psychographic segmentation when they sort their customers into categories of people who care about healthy living and exercise.
Psychographic segmentation is more complex to manage because it requires that brands acquire the necessary psychographic data from potential customers. In addition, tools are needed to manage that data and create market segments based on it.

Psychographic segmentation works by grouping potential customers based on their beliefs, values, lifestyles, opinions and interests. Brands use surveys, interviews and focus groups to determine the psychographic attributes of potential customers.

Examples of psychographic market segments include the following:

  People interested in healthy eating and physical fitness;
  P
  People who voted for a particular candidate for office;

People who practice a particular religion; and
People who believe in sustainability.

How do you identify market segments?

Broadly speaking, identifying a market segment requires the following three criteria. To start, the main needs of a sub-group must be homogenous. Second, the segment must share distinct characteristics. Finally, the segment produces a similar response to marketing techniques. Prospective buyers are grouped into various segments, often based on how much value they place on a product or service.

How to get started with segmentation?

Define your market:

Is there a need for your products and services? Is the market large or small? Where does your brand sit in the current marketplace?

Segment your market:

Decide which of the five criteria (demographic/firmographic, psychographic, geographic or behaviour) you want to use to segment your market. You don't need to stick to just one most brands use a combination – so experiment with each one and find what works best.

Understand your market:

You do this by conducting preliminary research surveys, focus groups, polls, etc. Ask questions that relate to the segments you have chosen, and use a combination of quantitative (tickable/selectable boxes) and qualitative (open-ended for open-text responses) questions.

Create your customer segments:

Analyse the responses from your research to highlight which customer segments are most relevant to your brand.

Test your marketing strategy:

Once you have interpreted your responses, test your findings on your target market, using conversion track ng to see how effective it is. And keep testing. If uptake is disappointing, relook at your segments or your research methods.

Market and opportunity assessments:

When your business wants to enter into a new market or look for growth opportunities, market segmentation can help you understand the sales potential. It can assist in breaking down your research, by aligning your findings to your target audience groups. For example, when you've identified the threats and opportunities within a new market, you can apply your customer segment knowledge to the information to understand how target customers might respond to new ideas, products, or services.

Segmentation and targeting:

If you have your entire market separated into different customer segments, then you have defined them by set criteria, like demographics, needs, priorities, common interests, or behaviour preferences. With this information, you can target your products and services towards these market segments, making marketing messages and collateral that will resonate with the segment's criteria.

Customer needs research:

When you know a lot about your customers, you can understand where your business is connecting well with them and where there can be improvements. Market segmentation can help with customer needs research (a so known as habits and practices research) to deliver information about customer needs, preferences, and product or service usage. This helps you identify and understand gaps in your offerings that can be scheduled for development or follow-up.

Product development:

If the product or service you've developed doesn't solve the problem of your target audience or isn't useful, then that product will have difficulty selling. When you know what each of your market segments cares about and how they live their lives, it's easier to know what products will enrich or enhance their day-to-day. Use market segmentation to understand your customers clearly, so that you can save time and money developing products and services that your customers will want to purchase.

Campaign optimisation:

Marketing and content teams will value having detailed information on each segment, as this allows them to personalise their campaigns and strategies at scale. This may lead to variations in messaging that they know will connect with audiences better, making their campaign results more effective. If the campaigns are combined with strong calls to action, the marketing campaigns will be a powerful tool that drives your target market segments towards your sales channels.

Perceptual Mapping

Businesses often seek feedback from stakeholders to recognize their strengths and identify areas for growth. Perceptual mapping is a tool that can help companies understand customer viewpoints to help guide business decisions. Learning more about perception maps and how to create them can help you optimize the use of a company's important customer perception data.

Perceptual mapping is a process of using a chart or visual representation to illustrate how customers perceive a brand or product. The map measures customer viewpoints and perceptions toward specific goods or services and depicts the feelings and impressions of consumers to help you understand their thoughts. Depending on the company's needs, a perceptual map can showcase customers' feelings about company products, positioning and competitors. When you create a perceptual map, you can use customer data from surveys, ratings and other analytical measures.

Types of perceptual mapping
There are two main types of perceptual maps: standard and multi-dimensional maps.
With a standard map, you may view customer data from a single survey with a two-axis chart structure. With this map type, you can often quickly chart two product attributes,

such as the taste and texture of food products. Perceptual mapping can also highlight customer perceptions of brand attributes, such as the quality and trustworthiness of a clothing brand.

Multi-dimensional perception maps may provide a more holistic view of an entire product marketplace with customer viewpoints on three attributes or more. This can include how different demographic groups may perceive a product or brand. It can also offer advanced competitor perception data. A bit more complicated, this map type may use additional statistical tools and require advanced analysis from an expert.

Who can use a perceptual map?
Any businesses and organizations that provide a service can use a perceptual map to better understand the perceptions of their customers. This includes the schools, colleges and universities that want to measure student sentiment. Political campaigns can also use perceptual maps to gauge voter perceptions. Marketing teams and brand managers often use perceptual maps to evaluate customer feelings in competitive industries.

How to create a perceptual map
Here are five steps you can follow to create a successful perceptual map:

1. Select attributes
Attributes are the variables the customer factors into their decision to purchase a product or service. Consider the most important aspects of a product and which aspects

you'd like to study. For example, key attributes for a food product can be its taste, texture, smell and quality, and attributes for a vehicle can be its price, performance and model year. You can select the most prominent attributes for your product or brand or select ones where you'd like to learn more. Select at least two characteristics that your average customer finds important.

2. Identify competition

You can identify the company's top competition, which can be several businesses or organizations that provide similar products and services. This step can help you develop a perceptual map showing where the company and its competitors rank in the thoughts and perceptions of customers. Try to consider which competitors are most compelling to potential customers and what you'd like to learn about how these competitors position themselves within the market.

3. Survey consumers

You can create and distribute a questionnaire that surveys a group of consumers. The survey can ask questions related to the selected attributes. For a food product, your survey could ask consumers whether they prefer their food to be sweet or bitter and ask their preferences concerning soft food compared to chewy food.

The survey can ask consumers to rate your product or brand on a five-point scale and to rate your competitors according to the same system. Whenever possible, try to gather more data than you think you need in case you run into any issues or would like to run additional analysis.

4. Analyse survey data

You can analyse the survey response data to see how the respondents rate your brand in comparison with competitor brands. You can review their preferences to see how respondents felt about your product or service and how they feel about competing brands.

The survey response data can show the preferences and perceptions of consumers. Depending on the amount of data and company resources, you can either analyse data by hand or use various analysis software or programs.

5. Create your map

You can create your perceptual map using computer software and the survey's data. Basic software programs can graph a two-dimensional perceptual map featuring an X- and Y-axis that intersect.

The map can show where you and your competitors fall on the chart that may depict consumer preferences for attributes like quality and trustworthiness. Advanced software programs can create more sophisticated perceptual maps, factoring consumer perceptions of multiple attributes, and may showcase how different demographic groups perceive you and your competitors.

Why should you use a perceptual map?

Some of the main reasons to use a perceptual map include:

Insight into customers

You can learn more about your customers and get a better understanding of how they view your product, brand or service by using a perceptual map. The information presented in the chart can provide you with insight into the minds of customers and can tell you how customers think of you and your competitors, which can help you develop or enhance marketing strategies for growth. Creating a visual representation of this data can help you better understand how well products ranks and how much room the company has for improvement.

Perceptions tracking

You can use perceptual maps to track how customer perceptions may change. Introducing a new product or service could influence consumer sentiment. By embracing perceptual mapping, you can track and measure whether the perceptions improve or remain favourable when introducing new products or services. You could also repeat this process if a new competitor enters the market. This could help you better understand how customers perceive the value of your brand against the value of other brands.

Market research on competitors

You can use perceptual maps to learn about your competition through market research by tracking and observing how customers perceive competitor products. Understanding customer perceptions of competitor brands and products can help you develop marketing strategies to better compete in your industry. Customers often make purchasing decisions based on preferences and perceptions, and those preferences and perceptions can provide you with an opportunity to attract and maintain their patronage.

Brand repositioning

Perceptual maps can help you reposition your brand by letting you know what customers think of your brand versus competitor brands. Repositioning can help improve the strength and value of a brand, and perceptual maps can help you develop an effective repositioning strategy. For example, you may learn that customers prefer competitors who offer healthy food options, so you may decide to showcase the nutrition information for the company's healthiest offerings.

Development of new products

Knowing what customers like and what customers prefer can help you develop new products that align with their preferences. Data from a perceptual map can help you predict demand for a new product, which can guide you in the production cycle when developing and mass-producing a new product. It can also help you learn how new product launches impact competitors and how you can integrate some competitor strategies into the company's product development and marketing efforts.

Margins

In the business world, the margin is the difference between the price at which a product is sold and the costs associated with making or selling the product (or the cost of goods sold). Broadly speaking, a company's margin is its ratio of profit to revenue. Margin is one of the most important performance metrics for businesses to track. A company can bring in enormous revenues, but if it has very high operating costs, its profit margins are likely to be anaemic. When margins are disproportionately low, companies must find ways to reduce costs or boost revenues to the margin which represents a greater percentage of their revenues.

The meaning of the word depends on the context in which it is used. While the definition above is most often encountered by business owners, there are others used by investors, lenders and traders.

Businesses are always looking to find the highest profit margin possible. When a business increases profits, the business has more revenue -- and that revenue can be shared with employees in the form of raises or it can be used to expand product lines or services, which serve to potentially drive even more profits into the business. Business owners use a variety of different strategies to f nd the highest profit margin.

Merchandise

Before a business can attempt a high profit margin strategy, the company needs the right merchandise. After all, trying to get a high profit margin out of something like an iPad would prove futile, since the only way to get high profits out of such an item means having to charge much higher prices than competitors. When an item is in short supply, however, it sometimes is possible to get the higher profit. In general, items with the highest profit margin tend to be the items with the lowest manufacturing costs.

Costs

To find the highest profit margin strategy, the businessperson must first determine the lowest cost possible to reach the breakeven point. The breakeven point is when the cost of manufacturing and selling a product or service is the same as the selling price. Once a business reaches the breakeven point, every amount over that is part of the profit margin. The more money between the breakeven point and the cost of the item or service, the higher the profit margin.

Efficiency

One way to increase the profit margin strategy is to find ways to lower the costs of producing the product while still retaining the selling price. For example, if an item sells for $4 and costs $3 to manufacture, there is a profit of $1 for each item. However, if the cost of bringing that item to market is $2 for manufacturing, the profit is $2 for each item, which is double the profit margin of the original manufactured item before cost-cutting measures take place. This is one way that businesses place such an emphasis on cost-cutting methods, since it is vital to helping to improve a company's profit margin.

Monitoring

An effective high profit-margin strategy means constant monitoring of prices and costs. By constantly checking the costs associated with the product or service and adjusting prices accordingly, a company ensures the highest profit margin. In order to retain the highest profit margins possible, prices should be adjusted whenever a company's costs change, when the competition raises their prices and when an economy experiences either a sharp upturn or a sharp downturn. When an economy has a downturn, lowering prices can result in a profit margin that is lower but creates an increase in sales.

Profit Margin

Profit margin is the measure of your business's profitability. It is expressed as a percentage and measures how much of every dollar in sales or services that your company keeps from its earnings. Profit margin represents the company's net income when it's divided by the net sales or revenue. Net income – or net profit – is determined by subtracting the company's expenses from its total revenue.

Profit margins determine how much money you are making and represent the overall financial health of your business.

Businesses need to pay attention to profit margins to remain fiscally healthy.

Profit margins measure how well a company is doing. A business owner should always know how their organization is spending money so they can optimize profits.

It's important to know what your profit margins are and track them at all times. Your business needs to make money to keep afloat, and monitoring your profit margins helps you know the health of your business and tells you if your company can grow. Whether you're a well-established company or a start-up working out of a garage, you should understand your profit margins.

In business accounting, there are different types of profit margin which need to be calculated and tracked in order to maintain a clear understanding of the company's financial health. Gross profit margin, operating profit margin, and net profit margin are the three main margin analysis measures that are used to analyse the income statement activities of a firm.

Each margin individually gives a very different perspective on the company's operational efficiency. Comprehensively the three margins taken together can provide insight into a firm's operational strengths and weaknesses (SWOT). Margins are also useful in making competitor comparisons and identifying growth and loss trends against past periods.

By analysing how the gross, operating, and net profit margins compare to each other, industry analysts can get a clear picture of a company's operating strengths and weaknesses.

Market and business factors may affect each of the three margins differently. Systematically if direct sales expenses increase across the market, then a company will have a lower gross profit margin that reflects higher costs of sales. Companies may go through different cycles of growth that lead to higher operational, and interest expenses. A company may be investing more in marketing campaigns or capital investments that increase operating costs for a period which can decrease operating profit margin. Companies may also raise capital through debt which can decrease their net profit margin when interest payments rise.
Understanding these different variables and their effects on margin analysis can be important for investors when analyzing the worthiness of corporate investment.

Gross Profit Margin

Gross profit margin analyses the relationship between gross sales revenue and the direct costs of sales. This comparison forms the first section of the income statement. Companies will have varying types of direct costs depending on their business. Companies that are involved in the production and manufacturing of goods will use the cost of goods sold measure while service companies may have a more generalized notation.

Overall, the gross profit margin seeks to identify how efficiently a company is producing its product. The calculation for gross profit margin is gross profit divided by total revenue. In general, it is better to have a higher gross profit margin number as it represents the total gross profit per dollar of revenue.

A company's gross profit margin refers to the profits the company makes after variable production costs have been deducted but before fixed costs have been accounted for. It is used to get an understanding of how efficiently the company is using its resources such as materials and personnel.

Operating Profit Margin

Operating efficiency forms the second section of a company's income statement and focuses on indirect costs. Companies have a wide range of indirect costs which also influence the bottom line. Some commonly reported indirect costs includes research and development, marketing campaign expenses, general and administrative expenses, and depreciation and amortization.

Operating profit margin examines the effects of these costs. Operating profit is obtained by subtracting operating expenses from gross profit. The operating profit margin is then calculated by dividing the operating profit by total revenue.

Operating profit shows a company's ability to manage its indirect costs. Therefore, this section of the income statement shows how a company is investing in areas it expects will help to improve its brand and business growth through several channels. A company may have a high gross profit margin but a relatively low operating profit margin if its indirect expenses for things like marketing, or capital investment allocations are high.

A company's operating margin tracks how much profit it makes on every pound in revenue after all variable costs are accounted for (including raw materials and employee wages), but before tax has been paid. It is important to track margin. Companies may be earning strong revenues, but if their operating costs are high, the business may still be in poor financial health. Therefore, the company can determine its profitability by tracking its gross margin, its net margin and its operating margin.

Operating profit margin accounts for operating costs, administrative costs and sales expenses. It includes amortization rates and asset depreciation, but it does not include taxes, debts, and other non-operational or executive-level costs. It tells you how much of each dollar is left after all the operating costs to run the business are considered. Here is the formula for operating profit margin: Operating income ÷ Revenue x 100 = Operating profit margin

How can you improve profit margins?

Your company's margins reflect the overall profitability of your business, relative to its gross sales. While many companies looking to grow focus their efforts on increasing sales, improving profit margins is another way that business owners can drastically increase their profitability. By widening your profit margins, you can make more from every dollar of your gross revenue.

Tracking expenses

You should always know how much money your business is spending. One of the most important steps in improving your profit margins is tracking expenses. If you don't know what you're spending money on, how can you cut costs and ultimately improve your profit margins?

Net Profit Margin

Net profit margin is the most difficult type of profit margin to track, but it gives you the most insight into your bottom line. It takes into account all expenses and income from other sources – such as investments.

Net profit margin is the third and final profit margin metric used in income statement analysis. It is calculated by analysing the last section of the income statement and the net earnings of a company after accounting for all expenses.

Net profit margin takes into consideration the interest and taxes paid by a company. Net profit is calculated by subtracting interest and taxes from operating profit—also known as earnings before interest and taxes (EBIT). The net profit margin is then calculated by dividing net profit over total revenue.

Net profit spotlights a company's ability to manage its interest payments and tax payments. Interest payments can take several varieties. Interest includes the interest a company pays stakeholders on debt for capital instruments. It also includes any interest earned from short-term and long-term investments.

The net profit margin of a company shows how the company is managing all the expenses associated with the business. On the income statement, expenses are typically broken out by direct, indirect, and interest and taxes. Companies seek to manage expenses in each of these three areas individually.

Your net income can also be defined as your gross revenue minus pretty much all of your costs – including COGS, operating expenses, interest and taxes.

Net profit margin is calculated by deducting all expenses outside of the cost of goods sold (COGS). There is more than one formula for doing this; however, the simplest way is to start with the net income for the period. This is found on the bottom line of your company's income statement. Divide this figure by your total revenue and multiply the resulting figure by 100. This gives you your net profit margin as a percentage. Here is the simplified formula for net profit margin:

Net income ÷ Revenue x 100 = Net profit margin

Gross vs. net profit margins

If your gross profit margin and operating profit margin are healthy, but your net profit margin shows issues with the bottom line, you have both nonessential operating costs and overhead you can cut. If the problem shows up at the level of the operating profit margin, your operating costs are more than you can cover at the price you're charging for your goods or services.

Margin call?

A margin call is a trading scenario where an investor needs to add more collateral to their margin account. A broker will issue a notice to the investor, who will then add more funds to their accounts, selling more securities if necessary to do so.

The Marketing Mix and the 4 P's

A marketing mix includes multiple areas of focus as part of a comprehensive marketing plan. The term often refers to a common classification that began as the four Ps: product, price, placement, and promotion.

Effective marketing touches on a broad range of areas as opposed to fixating on one message. Doing so helps reach a wider audience, and by keeping the four Ps in mind, marketing professionals are better able to maintain focus on the things that really matter. Focusing on a marketing mix helps organizations make strategic decisions when launching new products or revising existing products.

The development of a comprehensive, effective marketing plan takes into consideration a marketing mix that includes several areas of focus. Typically, the marketing mix refers to the four Ps: product or service, its price, placement, and promotion. This concept was developed in 1960, when marketing professor E. Jerome McCarthy first published it in a book entitled Basic Marketing: A Managerial Approach. Depending on the industry and the target of the marketing plan, marketing managers may take various approaches to each of the four Ps. Each element can be examined independently, but in practice, they often are dependent on one another.

Sometimes, the marketing mix can extend beyond the classic four Ps of product, price, placement, and promotion.

Gyan Shankar
Distribution Channel

A distribution channel is the network of businesses or intermediaries through which a good or service passes until it reaches the final buyer or the end consumer. Distribution channels can include wholesalers, retailers, distributors, and even the internet. Distribution channels are part of the downstream process, answering the question "How do we get our product to the consumer?"

The term "distribution channel" refers to the methods used by a company to deliver its products or services to the end consumer. It often involves a network of intermediary businesses such as manufacturers, wholesalers, and retailers. Selecting and monitoring distribution channels is a key component of managing supply chains.

Distribution channels are the path products take from their initial manufacturing stage to selling them to consumers. The main goal of these channels is to make goods available to final consumers in sales outlets as soon as possible.

A distribution channel, also known as placement, can be part of a company's marketing strategy, which also includes the product, promotion, and price. It directly impacts a company's sales, so it is needed to make them as efficient as possible. A distribution channel is a path by which all goods and services travel to arrive at the intended consumer. Distribution channels can be short or long, and depend on the number of intermediaries required to deliver a product or service.

The various channels of distribution play a critical role in a vendor's go-to-market strategy. If successfully executed, any distribution channel model -- whether focused entirely on one mode, such as direct sales, or embracing multiple outlets, such as multichannel distribution -- can open or expand markets, exceed sales goals and grow a vendor's bottom line.

Beyond boosting revenue, distribution channels can also broaden the portfolio of products and services available to customers. VAR, SI and MSP channel partners, for instance, often provide consulting, technology implementation services and post-sales support. They might also incorporate a vendor's product into an integrated IT product.

The final customer is focused on whether a product or service meets its needs. The customer is often unaware or unconcerned about the intricacies of distribution channels. Having a working go-to-market strategy with trustworthy distribution partners is important in supply chain management.

Components of a Distribution Channel

• Producer: Producers combine labour and capital to create goods and services for consumers.

• Agent: Agents commonly act on behalf of the producer to accept payments and transfer the title of the goods and services as it moves through distribution.

• Wholesaler: A person or company that sells large quantities of goods, often at low prices, to retailers.

• Retailer: A person or business that sells goods to the public in small quantities for immediate use or consumption.

• End Consumer: A person who buys a product or service.

Types of Distribution Channels

There are three ways to make sure a product gets to the final consumer.

Direct Channels

A direct channel allows the consumer to make purchases from the manufacturer. This direct, or short channel, may mean lower costs for consumers because they are buying directly from the manufacturer.

With direct channels, the company is fully responsible for delivering products to consumers. Goods do not go through intermediaries before reaching their final destination. This model gives manufacturers total control over the distribution channel.

With indirect channels products are delivered by intermediaries, not by the sellers. Who are these intermediaries? They could be wholesalers, retailers, distributors, or brokers, for example. In this case, manufacturers do not have total control over distribution channels. The benefit is that this makes it possible to sell larger volumes and sell to a range of customers.

Indirect Channels

An indirect channel allows the consumer to buy the goods from a wholesaler or retailer. Indirect channels are typical for goods that are sold in traditional brick-and-mortar stores.

There is difference between the Direct and Indirect distribution channels. Direct distribution channels are those that allow the manufacturer or service provider to deal directly with its end customer. For example, a company that manufactures clothes and sells them directly to its customers using an e-commerce platform would be utilizing a direct distribution channel. By contrast, if that same company were to rely on a network of wholesalers and retailers to sell its products, then it would be using an indirect distribution channel.

Hybrid Channels

Hybrid distribution channels use both direct channels and indirect channels. A product or service manufacturer may use both a retailer to distribute a product or service and may also make sales directly with the consumer due to the commissions paid to intermediaries.

Hybrid channels are a mix of direct and indirect channels. In this model, the manufacturer has a partnership with intermediaries, but it still takes control when it comes to contact with customers. One example is brands that promote products online but don't deliver them directly to customers. Instead, they nominate authorized distributors.

Three Methods for Distribution Channels

There are three different delivery methods for distribution.

They are concerned about who will be allowed to sell your products.

1. Exclusive Distribution

With exclusive distribution, intermediaries take the company's products to specific sales outlets. This is usually done by a sales representative. This means that only exclusive retail outlets will be able to sell the items to consumers.

2. Selective Distribution

With selective distribution, the company allows sales to a specific group of intermediaries who are responsible for selling items to final customers. An important factor in how successful this strategy will be is the reputation of the intermediaries since they have a direct impact over the company's performance. In this case, the intermediary becomes the real consultant for consumers, answering questions and recommending appropriate products for their needs.

3. Intensive Distribution

In intensive distribution, the manufacturer tries to place their product in as many sales outlets as possible. The manufacturers themselves, sales teams, and commercial representatives are all involved in this method. They are responsible for distributing products to sales outlets. This distribution method is generally used by manufacturers of low-cost products with a high frequency of consumption.

Distribution Channel Levels

Distribution channel levels describe how close an intermediary is to the producer or vendor of a product. With each intermediary added, another level is added between the producer and the customer. If a clothing producer gives products to a retailer to sell to customers, there's one level between the producer and the customer. If the producer first gives the clothing to a wholesaler to then give to a retailer and then to the customer, there are two levels between producer and consumer. Adding another level might involve placing an agent between the producer and the wholesaler, to help find the wholesaler.

Level 0

This is a direct-to-consumer model where the producer sells its product directly to the end consumer. Amazon, which uses its platform to sell Kindles to its customers, is an example of a direct model. This is the shortest distribution channel possible, cutting out both the wholesaler and the retailer.

Level 1

A producer sells directly to a retailer who sells the product to the end consumer. This level includes only one intermediary. HP or Dell is large enough to sell their computer products directly to reputable retailers such as Best Buy.

Level 2

Including two intermediaries, this level is one of the longest because it includes the producer, wholesaler, retailer, and consumer. In the wine and adult beverage industry, a winery cannot sell directly to a retailer. It operates in a multi-tiered system, meaning the law requires the winery to first sell its product to a wholesaler who then sells to a retailer. The retailer then sells the product to the end consumer.1

Level 3

This level may add the jobber, this level adds the role of the individual who may assemble products from a variety of producers, store them, sell them to retailers, and act as a middle-man for wholesalers and retailers.

Intermediaries in Distribution Channels

After finding out more about operation details, it's time to see who are the main intermediaries who take products to consumers.

1. Retailers

Retailers are intermediaries used frequently by companies. Examples include supermarkets, pharmacies, restaurants, and bars. Each of these types of businesses has full sales rights. Generally, product prices are higher in retailers.

2. Wholesalers

Wholesalers are intermediaries that buy and resell products to retailers. Wholesalers sell to those who are going to put products in their own stores. These intermediaries generally don't sell small quantities to final consumers, though there are exceptions, like supermarkets that sell in the wholesale model. Prices are lower because sales involve large quantities.

3. Distributors

Distributors sell, store, and offer technical support to retailers and wholesalers. Their operations are focused on specific regions.

4. Agents

Agents are legal entities hired to sell a company's goods to final consumers and are paid a commission for their sales. In this case, the relationships between intermediaries and companies are for the long term.

5. Brokers

Brokers are also hired to sell and receive a commission. The difference between agents and brokers is that brokers have short term relationships with the company. That's the case with real estate agents and insurance brokers, for example.

6. The Internet

To those who sell tech and software, the internet itself works as the intermediary of the distribution channel. The consumer only has to download the material to have access to it. E-commerce companies also use the internet as a distribution intermediary.

7. Sales Teams

A company can also have its own sales team who are responsible for selling goods or services. There is also the possibility of creating more than one team to sell to various segments and audiences if the company has a wide range of products.

8. Resellers

Resellers are companies or people who buy from manufacturers or retailers to later sell to consumers in retail.

9. Catalogue

Catalogue sales, as the name indicates, is when a salesperson is connected to a company and sells its products using a magazine. Salespeople in this model also usually earn a commission for their sales. This type of sales is common in the beauty segment, with brands like Avon and the Brazilian Natura.

Reverse Distribution Channel

What happens when consumers need to return items to manufacturers? Consumers need to rely on reverse distribution if they receive defective products or need to return clothes or shoes, they bought online that don't fit.

In this case, the consumer is responsible for returning the items and needs to find information from the manufacturer about how to do this. Usually, consumers find information about returns on the site for the product.

How to select the Distribution Channels?

Knowing different distribution channels, it is apt to know how to select the appropriate channel for your company. Here are seven essential tips to help you make this decision.

1. Benchmarking

First, you must look at your competitors to find the best practices they adopt. This kind of mapping is known as benchmarking. The idea is to figure out how your competitors are distributing their products and adopt a similar model.

2. Project Review

So, you have mapped out best practices in the market and identified solutions that could work for your business.

3. Costs and Benefits

When we talk about distribution channels, one important factor is the cost associated with them. Always look for the best cost-benefit ratio. To do this, it is not enough to have a vague idea of the costs. You must record all costs and analyse if the benefits of the channel you selected are worth it.

4. Company's Daily Routine

Another relevant factor is the business' routine. What are the projects, processes, and activities in your business? The distribution channel must be aligned with all these details. Otherwise, you might have logistics problems that result in product delays that damage your relationship with customers.

5. Market Potential

Before selecting a channel, you should also consider the market potential of intermediaries. After all, unless you choose to use direct channels, they will also be responsible for sales results. Analyse intermediaries' market participation, reputation, and performance to only then try to select the most appropriate option.

6. Logistics

Consider logistical questions like:

How will products be transported?

Is there security for when the products are in transit and/or

where they are stored?

Where will goods be stored?

What will be the delivery time, on average?

7. Location

Finally, consider the location of intermediaries, whether they are resellers, retailers, wholesalers, or distributors. After all, your product must be sold in the region where your target audience is, especially if you supply a spec fic niche of the market.

8. Pick up perfect

Not all distribution channels work for all products, so companies need to choose the right one. The channel should align with the firm's overall mission and strategic vision including its sales goals. The method of distribution should add value to the consumer. Do consumers want to speak to a salesperson? Will they want to handle the product before they make a purchase? Or do they want to purchase it online with no hassles? Answering these questions can help companies determine which channel they choose.

9. Delivery time

The company should consider how quickly it wants its product(s) to reach the buyer. Certain products are best served by a direct distribution channel such as meat or produce, while others may benefit from an indirect channel.

10. Multiple Channel: If a company chooses multiple distribution channels, such as selling products online and through a retailer, the channels should not conflict with one another. Companies should strategize so one channel doesn't overpower the other.

11. Digital: Digital technology has transformed the way businesses; especially small businesses use direct channels of distribution. With increasing consumer demand for online shopping and easy-to-use eCommerce tools, direct selling means more success for businesses. Rather than having to rely on relationships with retailers to sell their products, software and artificial intelligence (AI) sales technology allows companies to manage sales, and automatically achieve high customer relationship management (CRM).

Online advertising through social networks and search engines targets specific areas or demographics and social media networks are increasingly considered the industry standard and changing marketing strategies. If a company continues to use indirect channels of distribution, digital technology also allows them to manage relationships with wholesale and retail partners more efficiently.

Positioning

If you want to grow your business while creating deeper consumer connections, it begins with choosing a position in the market. By establishing effective positioning, you can ensure your campaign messaging and social media marketing are always an accurate reflection of your brand's mission statement. Your positioning in marketing must always be in alignment with your brand. Here are some typical examples of marketing positioning:

Tesla

Tesla position themselves as a luxury status symbol. Tesla leaves price out of its branding and instead focuses on the quality of their vehicles. Therefore, Tesla is a luxury brand that is more expensive than its competitors. In addition, Tesla automobiles are long-range, eco-friendly, and electric.

Tesla differentiates itself from other gas-powered luxury and standard electric vehicles because of its high quality. The company established a niche market for itself and a fun brand to match it. CEO Elon Musk has even built himself up as a Tony Stark-like character, and the company promotes its uniqueness through ads and quirky features, such as "Ludicrous Mode."

Starbucks

Starbucks positions itself as a trusted source of upscale quality coffee and beverage. Coffee consumption in the U.S has been witnessing a downward trend since the 1960's. Hence, Starbucks was extremely cautious in choosing its target market. Starbucks targeted office workers, from the middle to high incomes, who desired to purchase premium products.

The company wants to make itself the "Third Place" - the place between home and work, where customers could gather, relax, and interact with each other. So, they were vigilant about their quality control to meet the high expectations.

In most of their advertising campaigns, they often highlight their identity by showing the following value proposition statements:

    The best coffee
    The finest milk used
    Rich & smooth flavours
    Natural & clean
    100% recycled paper use

All of these statements in the ad give a sense to potential customers that they will undoubtedly receive high quality, clean, and upscale beverages they'll love. With such a successful positioning in marketing strategy like that, it's no surprise when Starbucks for years has been the top coffee provider in America. People can't get enough!

Coca-Cola

The Coca-Cola Company launched Mother Energy Drinks in 2006 into the Australian market. The launch campaign was professionally executed, and Coca-Cola was able to leverage its distribution channels to get the product into major retailers. However, the taste of Mother Energy Drink was subpar and repeat purchases were very low.
Coca-Cola was faced with a decision, to improve and reposition the product or withdraw it and introduce a new brand and product. The company ultimately decided to reposition the product due to already high brand awareness.

The biggest challenge faced by Coca-Cola was to persuade consumers to try the product again. The company changed the packaging, increased the size of the can, and improved the taste of the product. The relaunch of the product featured a new phrase – "New Mother, tastes nothing like the old one."

McDonald
It positions itself as a place to get quick and cheap meals.

Microsoft and Apple
They position themselves as a tech company that offers innovative and user-friendly products.

Dollar Shave Club

Its name alone demonstrates one of the main aspects of Dollar Shave Club's marketing positioning: its low cost. The company has focused its positioning on convenience and affordability, creating a relatable brand for the average consumer.

What is Positioning in Marketing

Market Positioning refers to the ability to influence consumer perception regarding a brand or product relative to competitors. The objective of market positioning is to establish the image or identity of a brand or product so that consumers perceive it in a certain way. For example:

A handbag maker may position itself as a luxury status symbol

A TV maker may position its TV as the most innovative and cutting-edge

A fast-food restaurant chain may position itself as the provider of cheap meals.

Simply put, positioning in marketing is a strategic process that involves creating an identity/ image of the brand or product within the target customer's mind. The process indicates how you differentiate your product/ service from that of your competitors and then determine which market niche to fill. A company's marketing positioning strategy is affected by plenty of variables related to customers' requirements and motivations, as well as by its competitors' actions.

Positioning refers to the place you want your brand or product to have within a particular target market. More specifically, the process of market positioning and brand positioning involves how you market your brand or product to consumers to achieve that position.

Positioning in marketing is about more than simply adding a category or speciality page on your website. With positioning comes a need to live and breathe that expertise - from generating content to conducting research and branding your company to appeal to your defined target buyer. Therefore, it's essential to create content on your website that provides value for your audience to build trust and brand awareness.

Why Is Market Positioning Important?

Market positioning is a crucial element of any marketing plan because it impacts all aspects of your business. When done effectively, positioning quickly informs recipients of all of your marketing messages and everything they need to know about your product, service, or brand. That's why positioning should be the foundation for everything to do with marketing.

Market positioning influences how your market sees your brand and how you present your products to your target audience. It's fundamental for consumers to make purchasing choices out of the complex array of offerings. It's how businesses can compete within a crowded marketplace for each customer's attention, preference, money, and ongoing loyalty.

Positioning is the single biggest influence on consumers deciding to buy. Good positioning entices prospective customers to find out more about your brand's products.

Great positioning entices existing customers to continue purchasing your brand's products. Therefore, positioning strategies should always be connected intimately to the whole concept of target markets.

Positioning in marketing aims to establish or sway how consumers perceive you to gain a competitive advantage. A great positioning strategy elevates marketing efforts to help consumers move from knowing about a brand to deciding to purchase a product. And as positioning can sometimes be subtle, it's usually easier to detect when viewing from the same angle as a consumer. For example, look at Burger King's brilliant advertisement "Why eat with the clown when you can dine with a king?". Not only does it suggest that Burger King has a higher class of dining experience than McDonald's, but it's also an excellent example of how positioning in marketing operates.

There are several reasons why one should consider making positioning part of your marketing strategy. With the right positioning tactic, you can create better marketing messages, shape your services better, and structure pricing plans so that you remain competitive.

Advantages of positioning in marketing:

1. Create a strong competitive position

Proper positioning influences how customers perceive your product or service relative to the competition. When you create a positive image of your product/ service in the customers' minds, you're likely to enjoy an ongoing market advantage. By doing this, you can claim your position in the competitive landscape, which helps you a lot to stay ahead of the curve.

2. Improve sales

One of the main goals of any business is to improve sales and revenue. Implementing a task management software can help businesses achieve this goal by enabling them to streamline their operations, prioritize tasks, and manage resources more effectively. By having a more relevant offering and communicating it more effectively, your company may be able to penetrate a new market, which can translate into new clients and additional sales.

3. Define a clearer target market

Positioning in marketing allows you to claim a specific feature or benefit and focus your products/ services accordingly so that you appear as an expert in the services. As a result, your value to prospects will increase significantly.

4. Make more effective decisions

Once you have the core message that ensures successful positioning strategies, you'll be in a position to make more effective decisions throughout the process. Clear positioning in marketing also drives effective communication, provides healthier and stronger relationships with customers.

5. Connect to consumer needs

Through positioning in marketing, companies have an opportunity to communicate the critical benefits that their product/ service offers. It not only helps to energize the product but also connects it to the specific customer that needs it.

Types Of Positioning Strategies

While there are a wide variety of options to consider, positioning strategies are typically broken down into three specific categories. These three types of positioning strategies are known as comparative, differentiation, and segmentation.

1. Comparative

This positioning strategy works by comparing multiple products or brands to create a competitive edge and highlight their value.

2. Differentiation

By focusing on any unique features which ideally can't be duplicated, a differentiation positioning strategy ensures a brand's products will stand out from the competition.

3. Segmentation

In situations where there are multiple target audiences, a segmentation positioning strategy focuses on the different specific needs of each group.

4. Product attributes and benefits

Associating your brand/product with certain characteristics or with certain beneficial values.

5. Product price
Associating your brand/product with competitive pricing.

6. Product quality
Associating your brand/product with high quality.

7. Product use and application
Associating your brand/product with a specific use.

8. Competitors Making consumers think that your brand/product is better than that of your competitors.

Perceptual Maps & Positioning Maps

Perceptual and positioning maps are effective marketing tools that help businesses develop positioning strategies for their brand, product or service. Both maps typically have two lines along the X and Y axis, with the end of each line representing the extremes of two key variables such as quality or price.

Once each line has been drawn and labelled with the specific criteria, existing brands or their products are placed on the map. Once you have decided where your competitors belong on the map, you can place your brand or product depending on which map you are creating. You can also create multiple versions of each map with different sets of variables.

As both of these maps look similar and have somewhat interrelated concepts, the terms perceptual and positioning are often used interchangeably. But there are actually some key differences between how perceptual maps and positioning maps are created and interpreted.

1. Perceptual Map

A perceptual map shows the positioning of how consumers view competing brands or dominant products within the current marketplace. It's critical to understand that a perceptual map only measures perception, as there is typically a difference between consumer opinion and market reality.

It doesn't show the actual brand positioning or your desired positioning goals, but a perceptual map is still very useful for market positioning. It helps visualise how consumers perceive your products compared to the competition. Businesses can also create a perceptual map to identify any gaps or opportunities within the perceived marketplace.

It's also important to remember that this map is created using consumer perceptions, and people often view things differently. So, a perceptual map may not always match the actual characteristics of a product or the intended image of a brand.

2. Positioning Map

They both have similar concepts, but the main difference is that a positioning map doesn't measure consumer perceptions of products or brands. Instead, a positioning map consists of different attributes essential for visualising the actual market positioning of competing brands or products.

As positioning maps identify where existing brands and products are positioned within the current marketplace, businesses then have a few different options to create positioning goals. They can either choose a position on the map that fills a gap in the current market, or a position where they are in direct competition with existing brands or products.

How to Create a Positioning Strategy

To successfully create a positioning strategy, you need to create a positioning statement. This requires identifying your uniqueness to determine what differentiates your brand or product from the competition. Plus, you also need to focus on potential customers in your target audience to see how they work for your positioning.

While positioning is often used broadly to describe a marketing strategy, it's more of an element of a strategy rather than the strategy itself.

Create a positioning statement that will serve to identify your business and how you want the brand to be perceived by consumers. For example, the positioning statement of

Volvo: "For upscale American families, Volvo is the family automobile that offers maximum safety."

Steps to brand positioning
- Brand positioning within the marketplace.
- Determine your current Positioning
- Identify your direct competitor's Positioning
- Compare positioning to identify uniqueness
- Develop a distinctive positioning idea
- Create a positioning statement
- Test efficacy of your brand positioning
- Determine company uniqueness by comparing to competitors.
- Compare and contrast differences between your company and competitors to identify opportunities. Focus on your strengths and how they can exploit these opportunities.
- Identify current market position. Identify your existing market position and how the new positioning will be beneficial in setting you apart from competitors.
- Competitor positioning analysis. Identify the conditions of the marketplace and the amount of influence each competitor can have on each other.
- Develop a positioning strategy. Through the preceding steps, you should achieve an understanding of what your company is, how your company is different from competitors, the conditions of the marketplace, opportunities in the marketplace, and how your company can position itself.

Day 4

Organizational Behaviour

Organisational behaviour (OB) investigates the impact that individuals, groups and structure have on behaviour within an organisation, and it applies that knowledge to make organisations work more effectively. Organisational behaviour uses systematic study to improve predictions of behaviour over intuition alone.

OB is about is what people do in an organisation and how their behaviour affects the organisation's performance. Managers need to develop their interpersonal, or people, skills to be effective in their jobs. It can improve quality and employee productivity by showing managers how to empower their employees, how to design and implement change programs, how to improve customer service and how to help employees balance work–life conflicts. Today's managers and employees must learn to cope with temporariness, flexibility, spontaneity and unpredictability.

OB interventions can help you better understand a work world of continual change, overcome resistance to change and create an organisational culture that thrives on change.

Networked organisations allow people to communicate and work together even though they may be thousands of kilometres apart. Independent contractors can telecommute via computer to workplaces around the globe and change employers as the demand for their services changes. Software programmers, graphic designers, systems analysts, technical writers, photo researchers, book and media editors and medical transcribers are just a few examples of people who can work from home or other non-office locations.

Gyan Shankar
OB Challenges to Managers

Foreign Assignment

If you are a manager, you are increasingly likely to find yourself on a foreign assignment, transferred to your employer's operating division or subsidiary in another country. Once there, you will have to manage a workforce very different in needs, aspirations and attitudes from those you are used to back home.

Working with people from different cultures

Even in your own country, you will find yourself working with bosses, peers and other employees born and raised in different cultures. What motivates you may not motivate them. Or your communication style may be straightforward and open, which they may find uncomfortable and threatening. To work effectively with people from different cultures, you need to understand how their culture, geography and religion have shaped them and how to adapt your management style to their differences. Managers at global companies such as McDonald's, Disney and Coca-Cola have come to realise that economic values are not universally transferable. Management practices need to be modified to reflect the values of the different countries in which an organisation operates.

Innovation & Change

Today's successful organisations must foster innovation and master the art of change or they will become candidates for extinction. Victory will go to the organisations that maintain their flexibility, continually improve their quality and beat their competition to the marketplace with a constant stream of innovative products and services. Dominos single-handedly brought on the demise of thousands of small pizza parlours whose managers thought they could continue doing what they had been doing for years. Amazon.com is putting a lot of independent bookstores out of business in many countries, as it proves that books can be sold successfully from an Internet website. Dell has become the world's largest seller of computers by continually reinventing itself and outsmarting its competition. After years of lacklustre performance, Boeing realised it needed to change its business model. The result was its 787 'Dreamliner' and a return to being the world's largest aeroplane manufacturer. An organisation's employees can be the impetus for innovation and change, or they can be a major stumbling block. The challenge for managers is to stimulate their employees' creativity and tolerance for change. The field of OB provides a wealth of ideas and techniques to aid in realising these goals.

Globalisation

Coping with 'temporariness' Globalisation, expanded capacity and advances in technology require organisations to be fast and flexible if they are to survive. The result is that most managers and employees today work in a climate best characterised as 'temporary'. Workers need to continually update their knowledge and skills to perform new job requirements. Production employees at companies such as Ford, Toyota and Holden now need to operate computerised production equipment: that was not part of their job description 20 years ago. In the past, employees were assigned to a specific work group, gaining a considerable amount of security working with the same people day in, day out. That predictability has been replaced by temporary work groups, with members from different departments, and the increased use of employee rotation to fill constantly changing work assignments. Finally, organisations themselves are in a state of flux. They continually reorganise their various divisions, sell off poorly performing businesses, downsize operations, subcontract non-critical services and operations to other organisations, and replace permanent employees with temporary workers.

Training

A clear chain of cause and effect runs from employee attitudes and behaviour to customer attitudes and behaviour to a service organisation's productivity. By training employees to improve employee-customer interaction, Sears was able to improve customer satisfaction by 4% over 12 months, generating an estimated $200 million in additional revenue.

Absenteeism

Absenteeism, the failure to report to work, is a huge cost and disruption to employers. It is difficult for an organisation to operate smoothly and attain its objectives if employees fail to report to their jobs. The workflow is disrupted and important decisions may be delayed. In organisations that rely heavily on assembly-line production, absenteeism can be considerably more than a disruption; it can drastically reduce the quality of output or even shut down the facility. Levels of absenteeism beyond the normal range have a direct impact on any organisation's effectiveness and efficiency. Are all absences bad? Probably not. In jobs in which an employee needs to be alert—surgeons and airline pilots, for example—it may be better for the organisation if an ill or fatigued employee does not report to work. An accident could be disastrous. But these examples are atypical. For the most part, we can assume that organisations benefit when employee absenteeism is low.

Turnover

Turnover is voluntary or involuntary permanent withdrawal from an organisation. A high turnover rate increases recruiting, selection and training costs. What are these costs? They are higher than you might think. A high rate of turnover can also disrupt the efficient running of an organisation when knowledgeable and experienced personnel leave and replacements must be found to assume positions of responsibility. All organisations, of course, have some turnover.

If the 'right' people are leaving the organisation (the marginal and submarginal employees), turnover can be positive. It can create an opportunity to replace an underperforming individual with someone who has higher skills or motivation, open up increased opportunities for promotions and bring new and fresh ideas to the organisation. In today's changing world of work, reasonable levels of employee-initiated turnover improve organisational flexibility and employee independence, and they can lessen the need for management-initiated lay-offs. But sometimes an organisation loses people that it doesn't want to lose. So, when turnover is excessive, or when it involves valuable performers, it can be a disruptive factor that hinders the organisation's effectiveness.

OB look at the following three variables of organisation behaviour:

1. Individual-level variables

The first level of our model of organisational behaviour is individual behaviour.

'Managers, unlike parents, must work with used, not new, human beings—human beings whom others have gotten to first.' When individuals enter an organisation, they are a bit like used cars. Each is different. Some are 'low mileage': they have been treated carefully and have had only limited exposure to the realities of the elements. Others are 'well worn', having been driven over some rough roads. This metaphor reflects the fact that people enter organisations with characteristics that influence their behaviour at work.

The most obvious are personal or biographical characteristics such as age, gender and marital status; personality characteristics; an inherent emotional framework; values and attitudes; and basic ability levels. There is little management can do to alter these characteristics, yet they have a very real impact on employee behaviour.

Individual-level variables include biographical characteristics, ability, values, attitudes, personality and emotions—as well as four other individual-level variables that also affect employee behaviour: perception, individual decision-making, learning and motivation.

2. Group level variables:

The complexity of our model increases when we acknowledge that the behaviour of people in groups is more than the sum of all the individuals acting in their way. Therefore, the next step in understanding OB is the study of group behaviour. Chapter 8 lays the foundation for understanding the dynamics of group behaviour and how individuals in groups are influenced by the patterns of behaviour they are expected to exhibit, what the group considers acceptable and the degree to which group members are attracted to each other.

3. Organisation System-level variables:

Organisational behaviour reaches its highest level of sophistication when we add formal structure to our knowledge of individual and group behaviour. Just as groups are more than the sum of their members, so are organisations more than the sum of their member groups. The design of the formal organisation, the organisation's internal culture, its human resource policies and practices, and change and stress all have an impact on the dependent variables.

Knowledge Management in OB

In recent years, it has become undeniable that globally, we somewhat lack the 'high-end', technological skills that are crucial for many businesses and large corporations. Knowledge is a remarkably valuable asset, as 74% of organisations estimate that effective knowledge management disciplines increase company productivity by 10-40%. With this in mind, it's not surprising to see poor knowledge-sharing practices cost Fortune 500 companies over 31.5 billion annually.

Knowledge Management is a set of tools, procedures, methods, practices, and desired behaviours that help an organization to be more productive. For organizations, Knowledge Management is known as 'Knowledge-driven Driven Business Management'.

Knowledge Management has a lot to do with the way that we behave and work, the culture which we establish, support and nurture – or even come up against as organization leaders. In some cases, you may need to confront or defy a "not invented here" culture, to support and make it safe for people to share the experiences of their failures as well as their successes. Knowledge management embraces all of this: processes, behaviours, learning, technologies, and networks. This is what makes it an interesting and steadily evolving discipline.

Every organization can highly benefit from their people sharing, innovating, reusing, collaborating and learning information. This makes it a good idea to boost knowledge management by implementing proper knowledge management techniques in your business so you can take full advantage of the benefits:

By obtaining access to the knowledge of the entire organization, employees can advance the quality and speed of decision-making. When making decisions, enterprise collaboration tools facilitate the access to opinions and experiences of different people with diverse viewpoints and judgements, which may contribute new and fresh perspectives to the choices made.

Knowledge sharing and cross-collaboration help to increase the value presented to customers. The organization can give faster answers or shorten the time it takes to improve a product or service. Knowledge Management enables and encourages the sharing of ideas, collaboration and access to the latest information. It also allows individuals to stimulate innovation and the cultural changes needed to evolve the organization and meet changing business needs.

Knowledge Management simplifies the operation of finding the information you need, or the people who hold it. It increases effectiveness and productivity and allows you to work better, reducing the tendency to reinvent the wheel.

No one likes spending their time doing something over and over again. However, people do so all the time for many reasons. Avoiding effort duplication can save you a lot of time and money; it keeps employees motivated, and streamlines work too. So, by not spending time reinventing the wheel, you can have more time on your hands to invent something new.

One vital differentiator among competitors is the speed of execution. Assuming that everything else is equal, companies that deliver sooner than others will win. By sharing knowledge and innovation internally, you can significantly reduce the time to provide a proposal, product, or service to a customer. Which translates into increased win rates, add-on business, and new customers.

It is becoming more challenging for businesses to increase their revenues as industries mature and competition increases. Creating new knowledge through effective knowledge sharing, collaboration, and information delivery can help stimulate innovation. If you achieve this and many of the other benefits enabled by knowledge management, you should be able to see growth.

Create a self-service Knowledge Base for your teams, customers & organizations. Competency management is one of the foundations of the new strategic HR model; it consists of profoundly analysing the organization's objectives to define what its knowledge, skills and attitudes are clearly. Many enterprise companies are using LMS tools as a way to manage the employee training and education process. Companies can use LMS technology to share online training modules and job-related educational resources that will help their teams optimize operations and improve performance.

DAY 5

Entrepreneurship

Entrepreneurship is part of our everyday lives across the globe, more of us try to set up a business than have children. In countries such as Australia, Sweden, Singapore and the United Kingdom (UK), more people start up than get married.

Each year, around 100 million businesses are launched globally. That's more than three startups per second. In the UK alone, a new tech business was launched every 30 minutes in 2022. Entrepreneurship gives a holistic perspective on the fundamentals of business practice At least 95 per cent of all businesses around the world are small enterprises. If you are a European, by the time you are 40 you have about a one in eight chance of being an entrepreneur. Even if entrepreneurship is not for you, there is a good chance that you will work for an entrepreneur at some point in your life.

Gaining a better grasp of how entrepreneurship works is an excellent basis for understanding how individual business drives economic growth Most new jobs come from new entrepreneurs.

Globally renowned start-ups such as Twitter (founded in 2006) and Instagram (2010), and many more to date have redefined, challenged and broken up markets. To name a few, Airbnb, Uber, WhatsApp, Instagram, Mailchimp, Pinterest, Netflix, SpaceX, Facebook, LinkedIn, Spanx, WordPress etc.

This ability to challenge existing business practices contributes to economic development. As early as by 2014, Apple's output was equivalent to 0.5 per cent of total United States (USA) economic growth. If it were a country, its revenues would place it somewhere between Slovakia and Oman.

What is meant by entrepreneurship?

The most common and popular academic definitions of entrepreneurship are those of Scott Shane and Sankaran Venkataraman. To them, *entrepreneurship is 'the scholarly examination of how, by whom and with what effects opportunities to create future goods and services are discovered, evaluated and exploited.'*

Their definition has four key assumptions:

1) Entrepreneurial opportunities exist – but are not known to everyone.

2) People have different perceptions of the monetary and non-monetary value of an opportunity.

3) Some people will choose to pursue these opportunities.

4) Acting on these opportunities results in both profitable and unprofitable outcomes. This definition argues that there is a 'nexus' or connection between opportunities and individuals. Opportunities exist waiting to be exploited; entrepreneurship is a process of discovery, evaluation and exploitation, and the role of the entrepreneur is to find new means of recombining resources.

On the definition of entrepreneurship, economists, psychologists and management researchers all have their perspectives. Entrepreneurship is an elastic term, meaning different things to different people depending on the situation. However, there are three key components of a good definition of entrepreneurship: the risk and uncertainty, the entrepreneur and entrepreneurial contexts.

Making *decisions under uncertainty is the first element* of a good definition of entrepreneurship. This is rooted in a crucial distinction that the American economist Frank Hyneman Knight (1885–1972) made between risk and uncertainty. He understood that we calculate risks based on experience. Weather forecasters cannot be certain whether it will rain next week but they can use their records to estimate how likely it is to rain. Equally, a poker player does not exactly know what cards their opponent holds, but they can determine probabilities because there are only 52 cards in a normal poker card deck. For Knight, uncertainty differs from risk because prior experience does not provide any useful guidance on how to deal with it. With uncertainty, 'it is impossible to form a group of instances because the situation dealt with is to a high degree unique.

If asked to think about what the world will look like in 20 years, our only options are to guess or just say that no one can forecast so far ahead. Without knowledge of what all the possible futures could be, no one can determine their probabilities. Entrepreneurs face similar uncertain situations. At the outset of their new venture, they cannot be certain whether it will succeed because their product, market and customers are untested.

Knight's distinction between risk and uncertainty has two main implications:

1. You cannot manage uncertainty, but you can manage risk.

2. Entrepreneurship is a process of transforming 'unknowns' into quantifiable risks. Central to this process is that the entrepreneur 'undertakes' (*the literal meaning of entrepreneurship from the French word entreprendre*) to bring forward solutions that solve problems that can provide benefits both to the entrepreneur and society.

Who is an entrepreneur?

An entrepreneur is someone who launches a business venture, typically in the form of a company that manufactures and sells a product or provides a service. Entrepreneurs are often viewed as innovators who identify a problem or opportunity and then develop a solution no one else has recognized.

"Entrepreneurs—either individuals or teams—actively scan the environment for opportunities or discover them as they live and work. They form hypotheses about what customers want or need and how they can deliver value to the customer."

An entrepreneur is an individual who creates and oversees the major business decisions of an enterprise, with many of the risks associated with that project falling directly on them should issues occur.

A popular definition of an entrepreneur is that it is someone who is involved with venture creation. This led Gartner to conclude that 'Entrepreneurship is the creation of organizations'; 'it is a role that individuals undertake to create organizations.'

Successful entrepreneurs don't just charge ahead with their ideas. First, they seek to validate there's demand. Entrepreneurs "recruit people and invest money to determine if customers will indeed value the product and they can produce and deliver it at an acceptable cost. They often find different, even better ideas once in the marketplace."

Entrepreneurial Characteristics

There are different views of entrepreneurial characteristics. Most of these stem from the thinking of two economists. They are Joseph Alois Schumpeter (an Austrian-American political economist, and; Israel Meir Kirzner an American economist.

Schumpeter believes that creativity or innovation is the key factor in any entrepreneur's field of specialization. He argued that knowledge can only go a long way in helping an entrepreneur to become successful. He believed development consisted of a process which involved the reformation of various equipments of productions, outputs, marketing and industrial organizations.

Kirzner's entrepreneur is a person who discovers previously unnoticed profit opportunities. The entrepreneur's discovery initiates a process in which these newly discovered profit opportunities are then acted on in the marketplace until market competition eliminates the profit opportunity.

Schumpeter represents a synthesis of different notions of entrepreneurship. His concept of innovation included elements of risk-taking, superintendence and co-ordination. Schumpeter viewed innovation along with knowledge as the main catalysts of successful entrepreneurship. He believed that creativity was necessary if an entrepreneur was to accumulate a lot of profits in a heavily competitive market.

The concept of innovation and its corollary development embraces five functions:

Introduction of a new method of production

Opening of a new market

Conquest of a new source of supply of raw materials and

Carrying out of a new organization of any industry

Introduction of a new good

If we look across, we find several applications of his concepts of five innovation functions.

1. Introduction of a new method of production: Henry Ford's introduction of the mass production line for cars is one such example. Another is gene splicing methods that cure inherited diseases by altering specific parts of human DNA.

2. Opening up of a new market. Current examples include marketplaces such as eBay, Amazon and Etsy, which have led to significant changes in how we shop. In the past, we used to go to shops to inspect and then buy things. Now we go to the shops, inspect what we want and then buy it from the internet.

3. The conquest of a new source of supply of raw materials or half-manufactured goods. The scientist, Andre Geim, has won two well-known prizes in their life. His first was the IG Nobel prize for using magnets to levitate frogs. He won this prize because it is for science that makes people laugh and then think. His second prize was for the discovery of graphene, a carbon honeycomb which is 100 times thinner and stronger than steel. For that, he won the Nobel Prize for Physics.

4. The creation of a new type of industrial organisation. In the non-profit sector, charities traditionally raise grants and donations to fund their needs and meet social objectives. Nowadays, a more common not-for-profit organisational form is a social enterprise. These are more likely to rely on generating profitable trading activities to support social goals.

5. Introduction of a new good or significant improvement. Driverless cars could mean anything from greater opportunities for personal travel for blind people to the creation of 'mobile automotive offices.

Entrepreneurial contexts

Context is important because entrepreneurship is not solely the expression of individual personality. When William Gartner examined the question 'Who is the entrepreneur?' he found it difficult to work out what an 'entrepreneurial' personality was. If someone has Schumpeterian 'supernormal qualities of intellect and will', does that mean they behave entrepreneurially when they do their shopping or feed their cat? Gartner suggested that instead of examining 'who' the entrepreneur was, it is better to work out 'what' they do in particular situations. Gartner suggested that the 'unit of analysis' should focus on entrepreneurial behaviours – how ideas turn into start-up propositions, how teams and organisations are formed and how resources are acquired and combined – rather than the dispositions of the entrepreneur. The emphasis on the individual neglects the wider social nature of entrepreneurship. Commercial opportunities do not exist in a vacuum. Opportunities do not just exist 'out there', waiting to be discovered by a detached and solitary entrepreneur. Instead, opportunities are socially constructed by people working together to give meaning to the identification and realisation of opportunities. Context also points to different types of entrepreneurship.

The self-employed

Estimating the number of individuals engaged in entrepreneurship typically means counting the self-employed. These people work 'where the remuneration is directly dependent upon the profits (or the potential for profits) derived from the goods or services produced'.

By a study a little more than one in-20 USA workers are self-employed. This rises to just around one in eight in European countries such as the Netherlands. In Italy, Korea and Chile, anything from one in five to one-quarter of the workforce is self-employed. In Mexico, Turkey and Greece, it is one in three.

Studies show that the UK and the Netherlands have seen rising levels of self-employment. In contrast, in the USA and Norway, self-employment has been broadly flat or has declined.

Studies reveal the differences between men and women self-employment rates in a range of rich countries. The biggest difference is in Ireland in term of higher self-employed men. Canada and Chile have near equal rates of men and women in self-employment. In Turkey and Mexico, women are more likely to be self-employed than men.

Entrepreneurial activity is higher in poorer countries. In general, the less wealthy a country is, the greater the percentage of the labour force that is self-employed.

Many self-employed people operate in hyper-competitive markets. Self-employed workers are often concentrated in sectors that have few obstacles to entry and only require a limited amount of start-up capital. They typically choose sectors where there are few cost advantages to having a bigger operation and are disproportionately likely to be plumbers, electricians, restaurateurs, doctors, dentists, hairdressers, gardeners and small-scale retailers.

Self-employment is a measure of entrepreneurship because it involves organising resources, identifying and exploiting opportunities and making decisions in dynamic and uncertain settings. Policymakers and researchers use self-employment as a proxy measure of entrepreneurial activity because it is one of the few standardised ways of comparing entrepreneurial activity across countries and regions. However, there are two reasons why it is a poor measure of the quality of entrepreneurial activity:

1. Some self-employed people are 'necessity entrepreneurs. They may have only chosen

entrepreneurship because they have no other way of getting work. Necessity entrepreneurs might not grow their businesses or be able to stay in self-employment for long. This is in contrast to 'opportunity entrepreneurs', who are motivated to grow their businesses.

2. Statistics on self-employment only count those formally registered as being self-employed. However, many people work for themselves without formally registering themselves as an entrepreneur.

Tips to be a successful entrepreneur

Everybody wants to be successful, but what does it take? There is a Simple 4-part formula that can change your thinking to help you become successful. If you look at it subjectively, it's not only about hard work, consciousness is also related to business success.

We divide it into four facets:

1. Organization

Here is an example shared by Bill Gates:

"Bill takes amazingly detailed notes during meetings. He doesn't take notes from top-to-bottom, but rather logically divides the page into quadrants, each reserved for a different thought. For example, it appeared that all his questions were placed at the bottom of the page."

So, first thing each morning when you wake up, note down your main tasks for the day, so you can focus on them. It may take only 10 minutes but can change your way of life.

2. Diligence (Hard work)

Hard work is 25% success. Rest is to be filled by organising, prudence, and perfectionism.

3. Prudence

Prudence is the ability to govern and discipline oneself by the use of reason.

Ability to make the right decision devoid of ego, pride or prejudice.

4. Perfectionism

You have to learn how to double-check your work. There is a law of diminishing returns when taken to an extreme, but typically, an ounce of prevention is worth a pound of cure.

5. Never stop learning

The business world is constantly changing and maintaining the newest trends is usually a challenge, even for the foremost seasoned entrepreneurs. Staying on top of what's happening in your industry may be a must, especially when you're just starting.

Reading trade magazines, newspapers, journals and blogs may be a good place to start but you'll also learn tons by attending business seminars or workshops. Taking continuing education courses or earning a specialized degree typically requires a bigger investment of some time and money but it's going to be worthwhile if it helps to grow your business.

6. Invite or take help

Launching a business may be a daunting task and thinking you'll roll in the hay on their lonesome is one of the worst mistakes you'll make. Having a network in situ before getting started can assist you in avoiding burnout and supply the motivation you would like to stay going. It also comes in handy once you need someone to bounce ideas off of.

One of the foremost important people to incorporate into your network may be a mentor. Ideally, your mentor should be someone who's already established themselves as an entrepreneur and is willing to share knowledge with you.

If you're hoping to improve your entrepreneurial skills while gaining professional contacts, consider looking for a mentor. Your mentor can be anyone you trust who has industry experience related to your career or personal goals. Mentors who have experience in the business and entrepreneurial field can relay their knowledge to you and help you grow in your career.

If you don't have a mentor, take a glance at your professional network to ascertain if there's another entrepreneur you'll learn from. Opening the door to a mentoring relationship could also be as simple as asking them for his or her advice on something associated with your start-up plans.

7. Have a different or new idea

Writing out a business plan isn't a requirement for becoming an entrepreneur but it can certainly help to supply some guidance when you're trying to urge your venture off the bottom. A business plan is actually a roadmap that shows you where you're, where you would like to travel, and the way you'll get there.

Even if your business idea seems fairly straightforward, having a written plan can assist you to stay on track. If you're not conversant in what goes into writing one there are many online resources available, including those provided by the tiny Business Administration.

8. Understand and know what you're selling

No two businesses are exactly alike but all of them share one thing in common—every business features a product or service they're trying to sell. Becoming an entrepreneur begins with knowing what it's you've got to supply that might be useful to somebody else. For instance, if your business idea centers around a selected product, it's vital that you simply have an entire understanding of what it is and the way it works. Knowing a product just like the back of your hand ensures that you'll be ready to handle any questions or objections your customers may have.

The same is additionally true if you're selling services. Whether you're getting to start a financial consulting company or a tree trimming service, you would like your potential customers to ascertain you as an authority. If you're planning on seeking out investors to fund your efforts, you'll get to be ready to prove that you simply know and therefore the know-how to get the ball rolling.

9. Find an audience suits your business

No matter how great your product or service is, it's meaningless if you don't have someone to sell it to. deciding who your audience is can offer you a way of how viable your business idea is. going to know the competition may be a good starting line for deciding who your potential customers are.

Take a glance at the sort of individuals who buy your competitor's products or use their services you would like to concentrate on basic demographic information, like their age, gender, legal status, income, location, etc. It's also helpful to see how they shop for your competitor. Some companies rely solely on local businesses while others make the bulk of sales online. Knowing who the purchasers are also as to where they are can offer you a foothold when you're able to enter the marketplace.

10. Communication

Every entrepreneur needs to be an effective communicator. Whether a person is a solo entrepreneur or runs a Fortune 500 company, they need to understand how to communicate effectively to all stakeholders and potential stakeholders that touch the business.

An entrepreneur must be able to communicate with employees, investors, customers, creditors, peers, and mentors. If an entrepreneur cannot communicate the value of their company, it's unlikely the company will be successful.

They also need to master all forms of communication, including one-on-one and in-person conversations, group conversations, written communication, and email or online messages.

11. Be flexible

Staying flexible is important for entrepreneurs who are constantly generating business plans. The ability to adapt to unexpected circumstances can help keep their ideas new and innovative by forcing them to look for alternatives. Being receptive to others' input or understanding that your idea may have to change are two simple ways you can practice flexibility.

12. Learn from others

Whether you're starting your career or you already have relevant entrepreneurial experience, learning from others is a great way to improve your business skills and help make your company more profitable. Try reaching out to any successful entrepreneurs in your life and asking them about their career motivations and advice. You might consider reading a book by an entrepreneur you admire or listening to a podcast that's relevant to your field in order to learn more.

13. Deliver quality

When you're generating reports for investors, creating products for customers or creating a business plan, it's key to deliver quality work. This helps others see your passion and dedication to becoming a successful entrepreneur. Consistent quality work will also ensure you develop a reputation for being reliable.

14. Stay updated

Successful entrepreneurs stay up-to-date with the world's technological and business advancements. Every year, companies may use new software and different techniques to continue gaining customers and generating profits. It's important to be adaptable to change, so consider adopting some of these advancements into your own business.

15. Set goals

Goals can turn your business ventures or ideas into achievable objectives. By creating a set of goals for your career as an entrepreneur, you can establish steps to help your businesses launch and grow. It may be useful to identify a long-term goal, and then work backwards by setting smaller milestones you can accomplish shortly.

16. Challenge yourself

Challenging yourself can be important as an entrepreneur because it can make some other challenges feel more achievable. For example, if you want to find startup money for your business, challenge yourself to create a business plan that would impress a highly reputable venture capital firm. Even if you're not able to present your plan to that firm specifically, you may create something very professional that can help attract other investors.

17. Trust yourself

Being able to trust yourself as an entrepreneur is important because it can allow you to make decisions and pitch new ideas without hesitation. Having the ability to make quick and smart decisions can help your entrepreneurial skills grow and your business succeed. Trust your intuition while also taking the necessary measures to analyse and determine the risks when making decisions.

18. Surround yourself with hard workers

It's beneficial to work with other individuals who are just as dedicated and passionate about an entrepreneurial career as you are. Colleagues can motivate each other to succeed through friendly competition and a drive for success. Whether you partner with these individuals or hire them as key staff for your business, surrounding yourself with hard workers can help boost your business' productivity.

19. Take action

If you find an opportunity that can benefit your entrepreneurial career or business, it can be important to act on it. Try taking quick and decisive action, whether it's approving an investment opportunity or accepting the help of a marketing company. This can help your business grow more quickly and continue to generate profits.

20. Understand your finances

Knowing how much money you and your business have available to spend can help you prioritize what's most important and how to help your company grow most efficiently. One way to do this efficiently is to create a budget and set up a time every month to review your finances. Consider hiring a financial advisor or other professional to analyse your finances and explain them to you in everyday terms.

Essential Entrepreneurial Skills

Especially in the earliest stages of launching a business, entrepreneurs are responsible for performing a variety of duties—it comes with the territory. Before you have an accounting department, marketing staff, and product development team, you'll likely need to perform some of these critical responsibilities.

Taking the time to develop certain skills before launching your business can drastically improve your chances of success. Here's a list of some of the most critical skills all entrepreneurs should have:

Communication skills, which you'll leverage daily as you work with vendors, investors, customers, and various members of your growing team

Organizational skills, which will empower you to work toward your goals efficiently

Time management skills, which will be essential throughout your career, but especially early on, when you have multiple responsibilities

Data-driven decision-making, which will enable you to make objective, measurable decisions about your products, services, business, and customers

Strategic thinking, which will allow you to discover opportunities and threats that guide business decisions more easily

Accounting basics, which will be especially important before you have a person or team dedicated to managing your business's finances

Resilience, because every entrepreneur faces challenges and struggles, and it takes resilience to bounce back

DAY 6

Strategic Management

Strategic management is the process of making decisions about their future in this complex and changing environment. Strategic management involves making decisions that define the organisation's mission and objectives, determine the organisation's most effective utilization of its resources, and seek to ensure the effectiveness of the organization within its environment.

Strategic management has two phases, namely strategy formulation and strategy implementation.

Strategy formulation is concerned with making decisions about:
Defining the organization's philosophy and mission.
Establishing long- and short-range objectives to achieve the organization's mission.
Selecting the strategy to be used in achieving the organization's objectives.

Strategy implementation is concerned with aligning the organizational structure, systems and processes with the chosen strategy. Strategies exist at different levels in an organization.

The hierarchy of strategies can be classified as

    mission,

    objectives,

    business strategies,

    functional strategies,

    and corporate strategies

The Mission statement of an organization defines its line or lines of business, identifies its products and services and specifies the markets it serves at present and will serve within a time frame of three to five years.

Objectives can be classified into long- and short-term objectives. Long-term objectives specify the results desired in pursuing the organization's mission and normally extend beyond the current fiscal year. Short-term objectives are performance targets, normally of less than one year duration that management uses to measure the progress towards the achievement of long-term objectives.

Business strategies deal with the mechanism of competing in a given business. This is narrower in scope than a corporate strategy. A strategic business unit is an operating unit in an organization that sells a distinct set of products or services to an identifiable group of customers in competition with a well-defined set of competitors. Business strategy is generally applicable to a single-unit business.

Functional strategies are still narrower in scope than business strategies. These include the activities of the functional areas, production, finance, marketing and personnel. Functional strategies must support business strategies, but they are mainly concerned with the "how to" type of issues.

Corporate strategies are established at the highest level of management and involve a long-range time horizon. In a stable growth strategy, the objectives, percentage increase in each year's level of achievement expected, and mix of products and services offered to customers continue to be the same.

The various attributes of a growth strategy are:

(a) The growth rate of an organization is not necessarily more than that of the economy as a whole but it is more than the growth rate of the market in which the products of the organization are sold.

(b) Organizations will attempt to postpone or even eliminate the danger of price competition in their industry.

(c) Organizations will develop new products, new markets, new processes and new uses for old products.

The facets of Growth Strategy include the following:

1. Concentration on a single product or service

This strategy aims to increase sales, profits or market share faster than it had in the past. Sometimes the sales turnover may not be as expected.

2. Concentric diversification.

It is a growth strategy which involves adding new products or services that are similar to the organization's present products or services. The products or services that are added must lie within the scope of the organization's know-how and experience in technology, product line, distribution channels or customer base. This strategy becomes more viable when the industry to which the organization belongs, grows.

3. Vertical diversification.

This strategy has two options, namely, forward integration and backward integration. Forward integration moves an organization into distributing its products or services. Backward integration moves an organization into supplying some or all of the products or services used in producing its present products or services.

4. Horizontal diversification.

It is a growth strategy in which an organization buys one of its competitors' facilities or gets into its market. It can be accomplished through mergers.

5. Conglomerate diversification.

It is a growth strategy which aims to add new products or services that are significantly different from the organization's present products or services.

III. Endgame strategies.

These strategies are used in an environment of declining product demand. This category of strategies includes leadership strategy, niche strategy, harvest strategy and disinvestment strategy. The leadership strategy means that an organization aims to achieve above-average profitability by becoming one of the few companies remaining in the industry. The niche strategy attempts to identify a segment of the declining industry that will either maintain stable demand or decline slowly. Harvest strategy aims to decrease investments,

reduce maintenance, advertising and research to cut costs and improve cash flow. The quick disinvestment strategy aims to sell off the business in the early stage of the decline rather than harvesting and selling it later.

IV. Retrenchment strategies.

These are used during economic recessions and poor financial performance of organizations. These are short-term strategies. This category of strategies includes turnaround strategy, disinvestment strategy and liquidation strategy.

The turnaround strategy aims to cut costs by using the following measures:

Change management personnel both at the top and bottom levels.

Cut down on capital expenditure.

Centralize decision-making in an attempt to control costs. Reduce recruitment.

Reduce advertising and promotion expenditures.

Fire employees if required.

Sell off some assets.

Tighten inventory control.

Improve the collection of accounts receivable.

The disinvestment strategy involves selling off a major part of the business which can be a strategic business unit, a product line, or a division.

Liquidation strategy involves terminating an organization's existence either by selling off its assets or by shutting down the entire operation.

V. Combination strategies.

Combination strategies involve more than one strategy at the same time.

This category of strategies can be divided into simultaneous combination strategies and sequential combination strategies.

VI. Functional Strategies

Under this category of strategies, there are four strategies:

Marketing strategies

Financial strategies

Personnel strategies

Production/Manufacturing strategies

Marketing strategies consist of activities intended to move products or services from the producers to the customers or markets. Financial strategies consist of activities aimed at acquiring funds to meet the organization's current and future needs, monitoring and controlling the financial results of the organization. Personnel strategies involve identification of human needs, devising proper reward system, mechanism of retaining employees, mechanism to match employees' competencies with the organization's present and future needs.

Production/Manufacturing strategies.

Production/operations function of an organization aims to provide products/services to its customers by using a combination of the following strategies to fill market gaps.

Timely delivery of products/services.

Flexibility in meeting customers' demand in terms of change in product design or change in production volume.

Quality of products/services to meet customers' specifications.

Cost-effectiveness in terms of low price for its products/services relative to that of its competitors.

These strategic alternatives form bases for the production/operations function. The selected strategies are translated into operations subgoals with desired product characteristics, process characteristics and customer services.

VII. Competitive Strategy

Every firm competing in an industry has a competitive strategy, whether explicit or implicit. This strategy may have been developed explicitly through a planning process or it may have evolved implicitly through the activities of the various functional departments of the firm. Left to its own devices, each functional department will inevitably pursue approaches dictated by its professional orientation and the incentives of those in charge. However, the sum of these departmental approaches rarely equals the best strategy.

The essence of formulating a competitive strategy is relating a company to its environment. Although the relevant environment is very broad, encompassing social as well as economic forces, the key aspect of the firm's environment is the industry or industries in which it competes.

Competition in an industry continually works to drive down the rate of return on invested capital toward the competitive floor rate of return, or the return that would be earned by the economist's "perfectly competitive" industry.

The five competitive forces—entry, threat of substitution, bargaining power of buyers, bargaining power of suppliers, and rivalry among current competitors—reflect the fact that competition in an industry goes well beyond the established players. Customers, suppliers, substitutes, and potential entrants are all "competitors" to firms in the industry and may be more or less prominent depending on the particular circumstances. Competition in this broader sense might be termed extended rivalry. All five competitive forces jointly determine the intensity of industry competition and profitability, and the strongest force or forces are governing and become crucial from the point of view of strategy formulation.

DAY 7

Operation Management

Operations management dates back to 5000 B.C. with the Sumerians, who tracked inventories, transactions, and taxes, and has evolved into modern-day services like overnight and same-day deliveries.

The term operations management encompasses planning, implementing, and supervising the production of goods or services. Operations managers have responsibilities in both strategy and day-to-day production, in either manufacturing or services.

The field is cross-functional, tying in with other departments such as sales, marketing, and finance. It's involved in product or service creation, development, production, and distribution. In effect, it connects dots along the value chain.

Operations management (OM) is concerned with controlling the production process and business operations in the most efficient manner possible. It involves the administration of business structure, practices, and processes to enhance efficiency and maximize profit.

OM professionals attempt to balance operating costs with revenue to maximize net operating profit. Operations management serves as an organization's engine room, and plans and drives manufacturing and services. Operations managers maximize efficiency, productivity, and profit, which are vital to a company's growth, survival, and competitive edge.

Most companies have an operations department with many employees and a large budget. As per a survey three-quarters of CEOs come from an operations background, which shows the importance of understanding how a company functions.

We can also see the importance of operations management in these aspects of a company's success:

Customer service

Product or service quality

Correctly-functioning processes

Market competitiveness

Technological advances

Profitability

Functions that a business needs to run effectively day-to-day, including:

Overseeing multiple departments and providing goals

Overseeing and streamlining processes

Balancing revenue and costs

Developing strategic plans

Production, logistics, and supply chain

The foundations of OM:

Planning: Operations managers must constantly forecast, plan, and adjust to optimize processes based on conditions.

Process: The production of goods or services requires having strong, repeatable processes.

Efficiency: Managers must troubleshoot bottlenecks, inadequate resources, and downtimes to create optimal efficiency.

Cost Control: Production is typically a major part of a company's cost structure, and you must manage it wisely.

Quality: Good quality control is necessary to maintain customer satisfaction and the company's reputation. Companies can greatly suffer without it.

Continuous Improvement: To remain competitive, companies need to have processes in place to consistently seek better ways of doing things.

Technology: Underlying all of these foundations is technology. Well-used technology keeps a company ahead of the curve.

Profitability: Executed properly, all of the above foundations lead to a strong bottom line.

Functions and Roles in Operations Management

Operations management includes a diverse set of functions and roles, which can differ based on industry and company size. To carry out these tasks well, operations managers need to be organized, analytical, creative, resourceful, versatile and have strong leadership skills.

Now more than ever, operations managers need to be tech-savvy to compete in a rapidly changing market. Technical specialization can arm you with the analytical and problem-solving skills vital to succeeding in this field. We've listed the major functions and roles required of a modern operations manager below:

- Planning and implementing manufacturing plants
- Managing projects
- Planning information systems
- Helping to design and develop products and services
- Managing inventory through the supply chain
- Managing delivery to customers promptly
- Optimizing quality control
- Conducting procurement and purchasing
- Managing logistics
- Managing transportation and distribution
- Managing and maintaining facilities
- Conducting enterprise resource planning (ERP)
- Forecasting for planning
- Capacity planning
- Navigating industrial labor relations
- Analysing the value chain
- Optimizing resource allocation
- Eliminating waste and bottlenecks
- Continuously improving processes
- Executing a company's strategic plan

Operations Management Strategies

Operations managers are deeply involved in strategy, in addition to their daily production roles. From designing and testing processes to facilitating interdepartmental collaboration, we have outlined some key strategy and tactics points below:

Data Use: Analytics are essential for strong planning, adjustments, and decision-making. Two common types are efficiency metrics and effectiveness metrics. Inventory Analysis: To manage inventory in the supply chain, ABC analysis (also called Pareto analysis) comes into play. This method divides inventory into three categories: A, B, and C. Category A has the highest value and tightest controls, and Category C has the lowest value and loosest controls.

Data Challenges: Data is often siloed, which makes it difficult to compare. However newer systems and setups make this process easier and help analysts and managers to examine data in new, helpful ways.

Process Design: Researching, forecasting, and developing a sound process takes expertise and energy, but the results can be lasting.

Forecasting and Goal Setting: The best forecasting often combines a look at historical data with an analysis of changing conditions.

Collaboration Among Departments: With good communication and collaboration, operations management can work effectively with finance, sales, marketing, human resources, and other departments.

Principles of Operations Management

A set of operations management principles comes from author Dr. Richard Schonberger. His 16 principles are:

Team up with customers. Know what they buy and use.
Engage in continual, rapid improvement.
Maintain a unified purpose. Involve employees in strategy.
Know the competition.
Focus.
Organize resources.
Invest in HR.

Maintain equipment.
Use the simplest, best equipment.
Minimize human error.
   Cut times.
   Shorten the product path to the customer.
   Cut setup.
   Pull the system.
   Improve the workflow
   Employ total quality control.
   Fix root causes.
   Manage visibility.
   Let the market know about your achievements.

Tips for Good Operations Management

Keep Current on Innovation Trends:

Operations management is concerned with the quality of a company's technology and people. "Take the time to listen to suggestions of tech-savvy employees; only use technology that is simple to use and engaging for employees at every skill level." "Invest in educating managers and employees on the goals of implementing new systems, and make sure to build in rewards so that everyone is motivated to learn and use new technology."

Encourage Effective Communication:

Make sure that you communicate processes, rules, and policies to everyone. Have a smart marketing plan and be up to date. Pattern your marketing plan after whatever is on trend. Do it as soon as possible, and use that concrete plan with a timeline until a new trend arrives. Have weekly reports of everything about the company. Then, from there, manage everything based on the needs of each category.

Collect Data Electronically:

Having team members write down their processing numbers for data collection can lead to inaccurate data and [will] not give you the results you need to run your operations efficiently." "Use report dashboards and rely on data and analytics. Determine what information you need to run your business, measure it, and use analysis to augment your process and continually improve your operations.

Be customer-focused:

Design your processes with the end customer in mind. Think about what they see as value and what they're willing to pay for, as well as how quickly they expect to get results.

Listen to Your Teams:

Field-level employees, internal sales, and vendors have invaluable information and know what is going on with your product or services and the competition. Measure and analyse. We are constantly examining our internal processing times and employee performance and measuring success rates. Measuring your internal performance allows you to exceed customer demand. Expand your network. Managers from competitive firms change jobs. A friendly relationship can become a key alliance. Vendor partnerships in developing new products or services allow you to grow your operations while controlling costs. Joint ventures that benefit both parties can substantially increase your knowledge base while increasing your speed to market.

Slow Down:

It's important to consider the side effects of each decision and how you relay communication to the team. People tend to like working for (and have higher engagement with) leaders who maintain a level head and aren't too quick to pass judgment. Be proactive and strategic. Leaders mustn't be reacting all day. The constant reactionary environment can turn great leaders into fire chasers, which tends to devolve their communication. Stay focused on the numbers. If something isn't working as it should, it's better to focus on the measurable data than on the emotion of disappointment or the result. When you can tweak a process and measure it along the way, you remove the subjectivity and remain objective.

Assign an Internal Owner:

Make sure every project has an internal owner, or it can go off track," says Wiegand. "Understand the key performance indicators that will drive the business. Just because you can measure it doesn't mean it matters. Protect the data. Operations managers have to safeguard the info. Consider leveraging infrastructure as a service, with hosting, security, and redundancy built-in.

Keep up with your Field: Read a lot. Learn a lot. If you're a logistics manager, connect with your tech people.

DAY 8

Competitive Intelligence

Competitive intelligence (CI) is the process and forward-looking practices used in producing knowledge about the competitive environment to improve organizational performance. It involves the systematic collection and analysis of information from multiple sources and a coordinated CI program. It is the action of defining, gathering, analysing, and distributing intelligence about products, customers, competitors, and any aspect of the environment needed to support executives and managers in strategic decision-making for an organization.

CI means understanding and learning what is happening in the world outside the business to increase one's competitiveness. It means learning as much as possible, as soon as possible, about one's external environment including one's industry in general and relevant competitors.

Competitive intelligence (CI) or competitor intelligence is the process in which a company gathers and analyses information about its industry, business environment, competitors, and products to direct its future strategy.
Competitive intelligence is the accumulation of data on what's happening in your industry. It can encompass your competitors' social media presence, brand positioning, pricing strategy, product tiers or even their recent job postings. Competitive intelligence is the output of transforming these individual data points into a complete picture of your competitors' strategies.

Competitive Intelligence is largely believed to be a critical component of building a successful competitive strategy and ultimately leads to creating a clear competitive advantage in business. With many businesses facing an increasingly competitive environment, quality research and market intelligence can often be the difference between a thriving business and one that struggles to keep up with their competition.

Competitive intelligence programs are used by both businesses large and small, to help give them an edge. Organizations with a clear read on the competitive landscape of their industry put themselves at a significant advantage compared to those who are not keeping up with market intelligence.

Competitive intelligence practices involve ethical and legitimate research and information-gathering such as studying a company's social media posts for specifics that might reveal the timing of a product launch. Competitive intelligence covers the entire process of understanding your competition and market conditions to help give businesses a competitive edge. This covers everything from doing SEO research on your competitors, to user-research, and more. Competitive intelligence focuses mainly on understanding the competition, whereas market intelligence generally focuses on the customers and users first. Both are critical in building a well-rounded business strategy.

Examples of Competitive Intelligence

Each business needs to know its external environment to operate successfully. That's why companies in different industries consider competitive intelligence in their strategies.

Since large companies have big budgets, resources, and necessary technology, startups need to adapt to competitive intelligence insights. This way, they can understand their customers and offer better solutions. Let's take Airbnb, for example. This company managed to satisfy the needs of clients by using technology and consumer insights.

Airline tickets. A great example of using competitive intelligence is the way airlines do it. They change the prices of their tickets every day based on the information they obtain. For instance, if competitors increase the prices on a certain route, this company will do the same to receive good revenue. Besides, airline companies track the actions of potential customers to make price adjustments. For example, they spot users who search for the same flight details several times and increase prices.

Importance of Competitive Intelligence

Competitive intelligence is invaluable when you're mapping out your next move. With robust data, you can predict where your competitors are heading and how successful they'll be when they get there–allowing you to stay on offence. Strong competitive intelligence analysis supercharges your strategy.

Data rules everything around us. Data sources like social listening, purchase history, site activity and user demographics are already invaluable inputs into marketers' decision-making process. Competitive intelligence research is just as important and impactful when used correctly. These are just three ways you can leverage competitor intelligence:

> Multiply your market understanding
> Set your benchmarks
> Make informed decisions

Competitive Intelligence Best Practices

Companies have to obtain customer trust and provide excellent customer experience, and high-quality products to be successful. However, this process takes time and effort and requires collecting data about competitors and customers to know what to expect. CI is the key since it allows businesses to gather and analyse the necessary information. In this section, we've prepared three competitive intelligence best practices.

Create competitive habits.

CI is a constant process, that's why it isn't enough to collect data once. When you share competitive intel with your team, remember to do it wisely. There's no need in sharing every new piece of information with little to no context with your sales team. Team members will spend a lot of time processing it, so it's better to analyse how valuable these data points are first.
Provide relevant insights.

The timing of the insights can sometimes be critical. For example, your company's team can face a lack of necessary data. That's why you should have a channel for internal communication to share your insights and different updates on competitors and customers on time.

Analyse your wins and losses.

Companies often don't know why they've won or lost a deal. They rely on accurate feedback from their sales reps, while it would be much more effective to interview their customers and see the notes in CRM.

How to Conduct Competitive Intelligence Research

Tips for conducting competitive intelligence research are as below:

Step 1: Identify your competitors

It's tempting to keep track of every competitor in your industry, but hone in on your top two to three competitors and let the others go. Your top competitors are those companies will have similar value propositions, a large market share and comparable offerings. Remember, your main competition isn't the largest business overall. It's the largest threat to you.

Identify direct and indirect competitors. First of all, you need to know your competitors. If you have a lot of them, identify at least your top five direct rivals. Afterwards, determine your indirect (firms in the same industry that don't compete with you for customers), aspirational (companies in the same industry that can inspire your business), and perceived competitors (businesses that can come up during the sales discovery process but don't compete with you). Understanding your competitors means knowing your competitive environment.

Choose the main focus areas. Once rivals are identified, it's time to determine the areas you want to focus on for data collection. You need to gather all the information you can obtain online and from your front-line teams. It's worth narrowing the search circle to process information more efficiently.
Gather the necessary information. During this step, you have to explore your competitors' sites, products, social media platforms, and content. Find detailed information about each of them.

Conduct a competitive analysis. At this stage, your manager breaks down the information and pulls out the main trends and the most important data. Afterwards, the information is organized in the right manner to convey it to all the teams. You need to create your competitors' profiles and continue to track their updates: changes in products or services and customer reviews.

Step 2. Set your goals

Pick a few focal points to jumpstart your strategy. Do you want to refine your marketing? Are you looking to create new products and features? Is it time to refresh your sales strategy? Having a concrete goal lets you know where you need a deep dive and where it's okay to stay surface-level.

Step 3. Gather your sources

If you don't prioritize, you'll have too much information to take action. Go back to the goals you set in the previous step. Look for sources that support those goals. If you want to refine your marketing, pay attention to competitor websites, social media profiles, whitepapers or ads. Things like job descriptions are important, but might not give you the insight you're looking for.

Step 4. Create a culture of competitive intelligence

Start by sharing competitor intelligence regularly. Keep different functions abreast of any major moves your competitors make and share scheduled updates on the overall landscape. Mention your competitive intelligence research findings in day-to-day conversations. After a while, it'll feel natural for your team to reference competitive intelligence consistently.

Share your findings. To improve the strategies, share your findings with stakeholders. You can do it by conducting a meeting, sending emails, or using an internal chat. Store data on a reliable platform so that your team can access it easily.

Use the information to let your company benefit. Make your data actionable for each of your company's teams. Your marketing team can use it to start new marketing initiatives, while the sales team can use this data to improve scripts and sales processes.

The best sources for competitive intelligence

Once your plan is in place, it's time to start mining competitive intelligence. Competitive intelligence is everywhere but your three best sources are your CRM, your sales team and social media.

Your CRM

Setting up your CRM to capture who your brand goes up against is a great way to benchmark against your competitors. During the deal cycle, you can document which competitor products your prospects currently use and who else they're evaluating. When you win a deal, you'll know you're competitive with both their previous solution and other brands they were looking at. Keeping score is a great way to measure your success.

Your sales team

Sales calls can be a treasure trove of information about the way your prospects perceive your competitors. Listening to recordings gives you a direct line of sight into how customers feel about certain product features, brand positioning and pricing structures compared to your competition. Plus, you can get some great pull quotes for internal briefings.

Social media

Social media happens in real-time, which makes it a great place to get up-to-the-minute information on what your competitors (and customers) are prioritizing. Checking out your competitors' content and audience engagement strategy can give you a serious edge and help uncover new opportunities. If you pair your manual search skills with a tool like Sprout Listening, you can get a fast, detailed view of how you compare to competitors in terms of social reach, share of voice and sentiment.

Tools for gathering competitive intelligence

Manual analysis has a place in competitive intelligence research, but some aspects are better off handled by technology. Finding the right competitive intelligence platform will give your strategy the boost it needs.

Sprout Social

Sprout Social has built-in competitor analysis tools that show you everything you need to know about your competitors' social media performance on one page.

Ahrefs

It's a powerful competitive intelligence platform. Their batch analysis tool is excellent for competitor intelligence, surfacing stats like domain authority, number of referring domains, estimated organic search traffic and estimated number of keyword rankings.

G2
With information on market segmentation, industries and user personas, G2 holds a wealth of competitive intelligence information.

Craft. co
Craft. co helps companies evaluate supplier risk, but it's equally useful for evaluating competitor intelligence. The platform makes financial, operating and HR information readily accessible and refreshes in real-time.

To name a few other Competitive Intelligence Tools are followings:
- Crayon,
- SemRush
- Wappalyzer
- Prisync
- Answer The Public
- Owler

While larger companies have may have luxury of investing in competitive intelligence professionals, small and mid-sized businesses may not have room in their budget. Many organizations will need to gather competitive intelligence in house.
Competitive intelligence information can be gathered using market research tools, as well as online searches, other data-gathering methods, and even talking to customers or employees.

Information sources for online and other searches

Company websites for insights into target audiences or shifts in strategy, product pricing, product benefits, and so on.
Company press releases for new product, staff, or expansion news.
Social media postings, particularly if the company begins sharing information related to a product or service that hasn't yet been introduced.
Going through the sales process of a product or service to better understand how a sales team works.
Online job postings, since the types and number of open positions could indicate efforts to staff up for a new product or category development.
Company information aggregators such as Dun & Bradstreet or Hoover's Online.
User's groups on social networks that include LinkedIn, Facebook, Reddit, and even a company review site such as Glassdoor.
Using a SEO or analytics tool to better understand your competitions marketing strategy.
It's also possible to gather relevant competitive information by talking to people inside and outside a company. The

conversations might be overt – "Tell me what you know about product X" – or they might be subtle, "Hey, what are you hearing from people with products like ours about what's likely to happen in our field?"

Throughout the process of competitive research, it's important to always remain ethical and play within the rules. Never mislead or outright lie while conducting research, not only is this unethical but there can be some severe legal repercussions as well in some cases. If you can afford to invest in competitive intelligence professionals to help you with the process, it can save you significant time and money down the road.

The key to competitor intelligence is that second word – intelligence. Information gathered however formally or informally won't help a company unless it is analysed thoughtfully or carefully. You can use the insights gained through competitive intelligence to improve your current marketing strategy and respond appropriately to the current competitive landscape.

People who might have helpful information include

Your salespeople might learn information about competitors when calling on customers or prospects.
Employees who attend particular industry conferences might be able to share unique insights into the state of the industry.
Vendors, especially those specializing in serving your industry.
Customers who might inadvertently or intentionally share information they've acquired about competitive products or services. Again, never mislead or misrepresent yourself during this process.

DAY 9.

International Business

International business relates to any situation where the production or distribution of goods or services crosses country borders. Globalization—the shift toward a more interdependent and integrated global economy—creates greater opportunities for international business. Such globalization can take place in terms of markets, where trade barriers are falling and buyer preferences are changing. It can also be seen in terms of production, where a company can source goods and services easily from other countries.

Some managers consider the definition of international business to relate purely to "business," as suggested in the Google case. However, a broader definition of international business may serve you better both personally and professionally in a world that has moved beyond simple industrial production. International business encompasses a full range of cross-border exchanges of goods, services, or resources between two or more nations. These exchanges can go beyond the exchange of money for physical goods to include international transfers of other resources, such as people, intellectual property (e.g., patents, copyrights, brand trademarks, and data), and contractual assets or liabilities (e.g., the right to use some foreign asset, provide some future service to foreign customers, or execute a complex financial instrument). The entities involved in international business range from large multinational firms with thousands of employees doing business in many countries around the world to a small one-person company acting as an importer or exporter. This broader definition of international business also encompasses for-profit border-crossing transactions as well as transactions motivated by nonfinancial gains (e.g., triple bottom line, corporate social responsibility, and political favour) that affect a business's future.

159 countries are currently members of the WTO. International business is monitored in detail by the World Trade Organization (WTO) and reported annually in their World Trade Statistical Review. The report covers every country from Afghanistan to Zimbabwe, and all significant business sectors in granular detail from air travel to waste management, as well as the more obvious agriculture, banking and finance, commodities and manufactures. Their 2022 update, published in February 2022, noted the following:

- Overall, the value of global trade reached a record level of about US$ 28.5 trillion in 2021, an increase of about 25 per cent relative to 2020 and an increase of about 13 per cent relative to the pre-pandemic level of 2019.
- Developing countries outperformed developed countries.
- China's trade balance (export surplus over imports) grew by 4.5 per cent, whilst that of the USA shrank by 5.2 per cent.

We live in a highly interconnected world and that is inevitably reflected in the way we do business. As such, it has become increasingly important to stay on top of business trends in today's global economy to succeed. And to do that, organizations need to have an understanding of how international business management works. This not only involves understanding the way other countries do business but also includes knowing the right way to interact with people from different cultures. Therefore, if you are interested in a globally relevant career and succeeding at it, you should know what is international business management and all that it entails.

International business refers to the trade of goods, services, technology, capital and/or knowledge across national borders and at a global or transnational scale.

It involves cross-border transactions of goods and services between two or more countries. Transactions of economic resources include capital, skills, and people for the international production of physical goods and services such as finance, banking, insurance, and construction. International business is also known as globalization.

To conduct business overseas, multinational companies need to bridge separate national markets into one global marketplace. Two macro-scale factors underline the trend of greater globalization. The first consists of eliminating barriers to make cross-border trade easier (e.g. free flow of goods and services, and capital, referred to as "free trade"). The second is technological change, particularly developments in communication multinational enterprise (MNE) is a company that has a worldwide approach to markets, production and/or operations in several countries. Well-known MNEs include fast-food companies such as McDonald's (MCD), YUM (YUM), Starbucks Coffee Company (SBUX), etc. Other industrial MNE leaders include vehicle manufacturers such as Ford Motor Company, and General Motors (GMC). Some consumer electronics producers such as Samsung, LG and Sony, and energy companies such as Exxon Mobil, and British Petroleum (BP) are also multinational enterprises.

Multinational enterprises range from any kind of business activity or market, from consumer goods to machinery manufacture; a company can become an international business. Therefore, to conduct business overseas, companies should be aware of all the factors that might affect any business activities, including, but not limited to: difference in legal systems, political systems, economic policy, language, accounting standards, labour standards, living standards, environmental standards, local cultures, corporate cultures, foreign-exchange markets, tariffs, import and export regulations, trade agreements, climate, and education. Each of these factors may require changes in how companies operate from one country to another. Each factor makes a difference and a connection., between information processing, and transportation technologies.

The Growth of International Business

The prevalence of international business has increased significantly during the last part of the twentieth century, thanks to the liberalization of trade and investment and the development of technology. Some of the significant elements that have advanced international business include:

The formation of the World Trade Organization (WTO) in 1995

The inception of electronic funds transfers

The introduction of the euro to the European Union

Technological innovation that facilitates global communication and transportation

The dissolution of several communist markets, thus opening up many economies to private business

Forms of International Business:

The movement of goods from one country to another (exporting, importing, trade)

Contractual agreements that allow foreign firms to use products, services, and processes from other nations (licensing, franchising)

The formation and operations of sales, manufacturing, research and development, and distribution facilities in foreign markets

The challenging aspect of international business, however, is that many firms combine aspects of both multi-domestic and global operations:

Multi-domestic – A strategic business model that involves promoting products and services in various markets around the world and adapting the product/service to the cultural norms, taste preferences and religious customs of the various markets.

Multinational – A business strategy that involves selling products and services in different foreign markets without changing the characteristics of the product/service to accommodate the cultural norms or customs of the various markets.

The Benefits of International Business

Participation in international business allows countries to take advantage of their comparative advantage.

The concept of comparative advantage means that a nation has an advantage over other nations in terms of access to affordable land, resources, labour, and capital. In other words, a country will export those products or services that utilize abundant factors of production. Further, companies with sufficient capital may seek another country that is abundant in land or labour, or companies may seek to invest internationally when their home market becomes saturated.

Participation in international business allows countries to take advantage of specialized expertise and abundant factors of production to deliver goods and services into the international marketplace. This has the benefit of increasing the variety of goods and services available in the marketplace.

International business also increases competition in domestic markets and introduces new opportunities to foreign markets. Global competition encourages companies to become more innovative and efficient in their use of resources.

For consumers, international business introduces them to a variety of goods and services. For many, it enhances their standard of living and increases their exposure to new ideas, devices, products, services, and technologies.

The Challenges of International Business

Today, global competition affects nearly every company—regardless of size. Many source suppliers from foreign countries and still compete against products or services that originate abroad. International business remains a broad concept that encompasses the smallest companies that may only export or import with one other country, as well as the largest global firms with integrated operations and strategic alliances around the globe.

Nation-states have unique government systems, laws and regulations, taxes, duties, currencies, cultures, practices, etc. International business is decidedly more complex than a business that operates exclusively in domestic markets.

The major task of international business involves understanding the sheer size of the global marketplace. There are currently more than 200 national markets in the world, presenting a seemingly endless supply of international business opportunities. However, the diversity between nations presents unique considerations and a plethora of hurdles, such as:

National wealth disparities: Wealth disparities among nations remain vast.

Regional diversity according to wealth and population: North America is home to just a small percent of the world's population, yet it controls almost one-third of the world's gross domestic product.

Cultural/linguistic diversity: There are more than 10,000 linguistic/cultural groups in the world.

Country size and population diversity:

There were about 60 countries at the start of the twentieth century; by 2023, this number grew to more than 193. This total comprises 193 countries that are member states of the United Nations and 2 countries that are non-member observer states: the Holy See and the State of Palestine.

Economic Environment:

The economic environment may be very different from one country to the next. The economy of countries may be industrialized (developed), emerging (newly industrializing), or less developed (third world). Further, within each of these economies are a vast array of variations, which have a major effect on everything from education and infrastructure to technology and healthcare.

A nation's economic structure as a free market, centrally planned market, or mixed market also plays a distinct role in the ease at which international business efforts can take place. For example, free market economies allow international business activities to take place with little interference. On the opposite end of the spectrum, centrally planned economies are government-controlled. Although most countries now function as free-market economies, China—the world's most populous country— remains a centrally planned economy.

Political Environment:

The political environment of international business refers to the relationship between government and business, as well as the political risk of a nation. Therefore, companies involved in international business must expect to deal with different types of governments, such as multi-party democracies, one-party states, dictatorships, and constitutional monarchies.

Some governments may view foreign businesses as positive, while other governments may view them as exploitative. Because international companies rely on the goodwill of the government, international business must take the political structure of the foreign government into consideration.

International firms must also consider the degree of political risk in a foreign location; in other words, the likelihood of major governmental changes taking place. Just a few of the issues of unstable governments that international companies must consider include riots, revolutions, war, and terrorism.

Cultural Environment:

The cultural environment of a foreign nation remains a critical component of the international business environment, yet it is one of the most difficult to understand. The cultural environment of a foreign nation involves commonly shared beliefs and values, formed by factors such as language, religion, geographic location, government, history, and education.

It is common for many international firms to conduct a cultural analysis of a foreign nation as to better understand these factors and how they affect international business efforts.

Competitive Environment:

To ensure success in a foreign market, international businesses must understand the many factors that affect the competitive environment and effectively assess their impact. The competitive environment is constantly changing according to the economic, political, and cultural environments. Competition may exist from a variety of sources, and the nature of competition may change from place to place. It may be encouraged or discouraged in favour of cooperation, and the relationship between buyers and sellers may be friendly or hostile. The level of technological innovation is also an important aspect of the competitive environment as firms compete for access to the newest technology.

Strategies to Success in International Business

According to 2022 data from the U.S. Bureau of Labor Statistics, approximately 20% of new businesses fail during the first two years of being open, 49% during the first five years, and 65% during the first 10 years. Only 25% of new businesses make it to 15 years or more. If you want to be among that 25%, rigorous attention to these nine tips is a good start, but certainly not exhaustive. Being a business owner means being in a state of constant learning and adapting.

Gaining footage in international markets is one step closer for any business going global. There are a lot of benefits that come with such growth, ranging from the increased customer base to accessing cost-friendly talents and finding potential opportunities to dive in other markets. Managing an international business, however, comes with its own unique challenges. Business owners must then focus on strategies that guarantee continued success if they are to survive. Here are a few strategies that can help your international business remain successful.

1. Hire through PEO or EOR

Talking of challenges that international businesses face, one is managing an international team. Each company has its own labour laws and legal processes, which can be complex for any foreign business. These can sometimes take off the precious time that can be used in growing the business.

If you want to create an international team without the complexities of compliance, consider leveraging local employment solutions providers. If your business is in Singapore, for example, use Singapore employer of records such as Singapore EOR or Singapore PEO to hire local talents. Such bodies take up all HR matters for your team, leaving you ample time to drive growth for your business.

2. Seek to bridge the cultural difference

Another challenge international businesses face is the difference in culture. If a business is to be successful internationally, bridging the cultural differences is a strategy it must adopt. You may find that a product that is loved in your home country differs from the preferences of the international market. That is why it is critical to localize your products so that they are in line with the local culture in that country. In addition to localizing the products, it is best to adjust to the local method of marketing. Build a marketing strategy that will appeal to the locals by incorporating their culture, their language and their people.

3. Keep things simple

Most businesses fail in foreign markets to try to scale up at a rapid speed. However, starting a business in a foreign country should be taken the same as when you were starting the entire business. Keep things simple and expand as you go. Have a growth strategic plan in hand to give you direction. Stick to the budget and identify areas that you can cut back on expenses. For instance, consider hiring independent contractors or part-timers with a variety of skills to cut back on labour costs. Instead of registering a legal entity in Singapore, consider using Singapore EOR or Singapore PEO to establish operations in that country. You will save a lot of money and time that you could have used in registering a business there.

4. Partner with local experts

Establishing a business in a foreign country demands that you understand the tax laws and other local regulations. This has to be done right from the beginning to prevent legal and taxation problems down the line. In addition, laws keep changing; and it might bypass you since you have another business to manage at home.

If you want to succeed and keep growing in a foreign country, you must have local experts who understand the ins and outs of the laws. They will be on top of things whenever an unforeseen change is done. You will be able to manage the business better if you know that taxation and legal matters are in the hands of local experts.

5. Commit personal time to the business

Having reliable experts running your business doesn't mean you staying at home and letting things happen. You have to be willing to get in the dirt and get things done. That means that travelling to foreign markets is inevitable for you. Getting firsthand information on challenges they are facing will give you insights on how to solve them. You will also get the opportunity to create valuable networks that can come in handy for future growth opportunities. You must create a budget for business travel if you are to remain successful.

Thus, international business can remain successful with the above strategies but having the right entrance into foreign markets can sustain it. Ensure that you get it right from the word go; have an agile growth strategic plan and a realistic budget. Work on the insurance, legal and taxation matters, hire reliable talents and seek to incorporate the new culture in your business model.

6. Acquiring Market Knowledge

To succeed in a new geography, businesses must conduct due diligence to develop market insights. After all, a one-size-fits-all model doesn't work out well for an aspiring global company. Understanding the nuances of the local language, customer requirements and preferences, cultural differences, regulatory frameworks, and industry operations can help you devise the best strategy for long-term business success, growth, and scale in a new market.

7. Mapping Market Size, Product Segmentation and Opportunity Analysis. Once you have acquired the knowledge about the chosen market, the next step is to select the best approach to successfully crack it. Determining the market size, mapping its future growth potential, and analysing the competition should be the top priorities, as these insights can help you gauge how much time and resources you need to invest to drive optimum value.

It is also important to identify and segregate existing market challenges on a granular level, and how they can be turned into opportunities. Such in-depth analysis allows you to develop highly customised products/services to reach out to each target consumer demographic, thus maximising your revenue opportunities.

8. Prospective Regulatory and Legal Impact on the Business

Depending on your industry, you might have to face unique regulatory and legal challenges when expanding into another country. All these cannot be ignored, for your business will have to operate within the regulatory and legal framework of the target market. You will have to address aspects like labour and employment laws, investment and business procedures, corporate organization practices, dispute resolution, trademark requirements, customs laws, regulatory requirements and much more.

While meeting all these criteria before officially launching your business in a new country can be a complex process, there are plenty of resources available to help you understand these nuances and get started. It is always advisable to seek experienced legal guidance for foreign business practices to identify threats and risks that may act as a barrier to your business.

9. Identifying the Right Partners

When planning to enter a new country, you may need to create a separate team to manage the regional operations in terms of distribution, logistics, dispute resolution, governance, taxation, and finances. Doing so at competitive speed and scale will need you to rely on local businesses with expertise in these critical functions.

You may also need to explore local alliances and partnerships by joining forces with other companies, of similar size and market presence, located in the territory you are entering. Such partnerships will enable you to test the waters while minimising your risk exposure, as well as to gain access to local expertise, business networks, and established supply chains, making it one of the most effective ways to grow your business in newer markets.

10. Build a Robust Go-to-market (GTM) Strategy

A go-to-market strategy is created to focus specifically on delivering a product or service to the end customer. To create a winning GTM strategy, you must first define the target market, followed by secondary research on the market size, its growth potential, and internal dynamics.

Once the target market has been outlined, you must analyse potential customers and their various requirements to identify how your organisation can best serve them. A strong positioning strategy can accordingly be devised to highlight your business's USP and to build its brand salience among your target audiences.

No doubt expanding internationally involves many intricacies and risks. However vigilant and meticulous planning, optimised resource allocation, and realistic expectation-setting can help maximize your chances of setting up a successful global business.

Skills Needed for Success in International Business

To thrive in the world of international business today demands an entirely different set of skills than was expected even a decade ago. Now more than ever, global professionals face a "VUCA" business environment—one that's volatile, uncertain, complex, and ambiguous. The skills needed to navigate this new, globalized business landscape aren't the "hard skills" of, say, analysis or accounting. While strong technical know-how is still essential, it's the "soft skills" that can mean the difference between survival and true success in international business.

In a study on 100 of the world's leading CEOs on what key competencies business graduates need when it comes to international business skills, they confirmed that soft skills in areas like influencing, collaborating, and thinking adaptively were critical for employability and success. They identified the top following 7 skills needed for success in international business. Whether you're hoping to land a job at a top multinational company, seek a new career abroad, or launch your own business venture, these are the skills that you need to succeed:

- Cross-cultural communication skills
- Excellent networking abilities
- Collaboration
- Interpersonal influence
- Adaptive thinking
- Emotional intelligence
- Resilience

Cross-cultural communication skills

Any role or function in international business means working in diverse workplace with people from a different country or background to yours. Whether they're a colleague, a client, or a customer, understanding how to communicate across cultures is an absolutely indispensable skill.

It requires no small amount of sensitivity, respect, and diplomacy. It also requires an open mind and, often, a little bit of research. Make an effort to learn, understand, and appreciate cultural differences and nuances when it comes to communication. Knowing, for instance, how people from other cultures interpret workplace confrontation or something as simple as maintaining eye contact can help to avoid misunderstandings and facilitate better workplace communication. Good communication is good for business. Studies suggest that a communication breakdown is one of the top reasons why projects fail.

Of course, listening skills are an often overlooked element of effective communication. When you're working with colleagues or customers abroad, actively listening is more important than ever, especially if there is a language barrier.

Excellent networking abilities

If you want to work in international business, developing a strong network of connections outside of your home country is essential. Successful networking can open the door to unexpected business opportunities overseas, and some reports claim that up to 80% of jobs are now landed through networking.

While online platforms like LinkedIn make it easier to find and maintain professional connections abroad, excellent in-person networking ability is still among the key skills for success in international business. Mastering your "elevator pitch" and attending industry networking events is one useful way to meet like-minded professionals and grow your connections. Of course, like cross-cultural communication, networking skills also require diplomacy, tact, and a listening ear—remember that you're building a relationship rather than simply selling your skills.

For ambitious international business professionals, one of the most valuable networking opportunities is often going to business school. From your peers to your professors, the people you'll meet in an MBA or Executive MBA program will come from all over the world and boast a diverse range of skills and expertise, making them strong candidates as future collaborators or colleagues.

Collaboration

For success in international business, it's not enough to simply build a network — you need to work well with others. The ability to collaborate and work together for a common purpose is fundamental in the business world. It requires humility, allowing others to take the lead and share credit for success. It also requires confidence to tackle problems, give and receive feedback, and respectfully fight your cause.

In an international business environment, collaborating with team members from other cultures is especially beneficial. First, it's an opportunity to use and develop your cross-cultural communication skills. Secondly, it will expose you to new perspectives and ways of addressing difficult business problems. The most inspiring and successful business leaders are often the best collaborators, knowing that collective brainpower can accelerate company success.

Interpersonal influence

The ability to influence others is fundamental to business success, whether you're trying to persuade an investor to secure funding for your new venture, encourage an employee to adopt a new way of working, or convince a customer to buy your product. The best business leaders gain influence by developing good professional relationships and building respect — meaning communication, networking, and collaboration can all culminate in influence.

Mastering interpersonal influence eliminates the need for a hard sell, encouraging others to get on board with your ideas because they understand the value you offer. It's the ability to be assertive, without being aggressive. In international business, it's a skill that will serve you well in pitching for new business, negotiating deals, and motivating diverse teams.

Adaptive thinking

In today's VUCA business environment, you must have the confidence to react and adapt quickly, thinking "out of the box" to solve problems. Adaptive thinkers thrive in an ever-changing environment, making them well placed for success in international business. But how can you develop adaptive thinking skills?

Emotional intelligence

In today's HR terms, you're more likely to hear people valuing "EQ" over the more traditional measure of "IQ". Strong emotional intelligence is noted as a critical skill when it comes to how to do international business. That's because it influences nearly every aspect of business interaction.

Emotionally intelligent people are self-aware and in control of their emotions, meaning they are better able to react calmly in critical or stressful business situations and adapt flexibly to change. They are also able to work together effectively, collaborating and communicating well thanks to above-average interpersonal skills and a strong sense of empathy.

To help develop the valuable professional skills associated with strong emotional intelligence, a research team from Ashridge Executive Education at Hult International Business School is investigating the role mindfulness practice can play in leadership training.

Resilience

Going hand-in-hand with emotional intelligence, resilience is a key characteristic for success, allowing you to rise to meet the inevitable challenges of global business, maintain motivation, overcome risks, and recover quickly from hardship. To succeed in international business unequivocally demands mental toughness and resilience. On a practical level, working across time zones and cultures involves long hours. Failure and setbacks are also a fact of life in the business world, but defeat isn't. This is where resilience comes in.

Get Organized

To achieve business success, you need to be organized. It will help you complete tasks and stay on top of things to be done. A good way to be organized is to create a to-do list each day. As you complete each item, check it off your list. This will ensure that you're not forgetting anything and completing all the tasks that are essential to the survival of your business.

Many software-as-a-service (SaaS) tools exist to increase organization. Tools like Slack, Asana, Zoom, Microscft Teams, and other newer additions.1234 That being said, a simple Excel spreadsheet will meet many of a business's organization requirements.

Keep Detailed Records

All successful businesses keep detailed records. By doing so, you'll know where the business stands financially and what potential challenges you could be facing. Just knowing this gives you time to create strategies to overcome those challenges.

Most businesses are choosing to keep two sets of records: one physical and one in the cloud. By having records that are constantly uploaded and backed up, a business no longer has to worry about losing their data. The physical record exists as a backup but more often than not, it is used to ensure that the other information is correct.

Analyse Your Competition

Competition breeds the best results. To be successful, you can't be afraid to study and learn from your competitors. After all, they may be doing something right that you can implement in your business to make more money.

How you analyse competition will vary between sectors. If you're a restaurant owner, you may simply be able to dine at your competition's restaurants, ask other customers what they think, and gain information that way. However, you could be a company with much more limited access to your competitors, such as a chemicals company. In that case, you would work with a business professional and accountant to go over not just what the business presents to the world, but any financial information you may be able to get on the company as well.

Understand the Risks and Rewards

The key to being successful is taking calculated risks to help your business grow. A good question to ask is "What's the downside?" If you can answer this question, then you know what the worst-case scenario is. This knowledge will allow you to take the kinds of calculated risks that can generate tremendous rewards.

Understanding risks and rewards includes being smart about the timing of starting your business. For example, did the severe economic dislocation of 2020 provide you with an opportunity (say, manufacturing and selling face masks) or an impediment (such as opening a new restaurant during constraints on indoor dining)?56

Be Creative

Always be looking for ways to improve your business and make it stand out from the competition. Recognize that you don't know everything and be open to new ideas and different approaches to your business.

There are many outlets that may lead to additional revenues. Take Amazon for example. The company started out as a bookseller and grew into an eCommerce giant. Not a lot of people expected that one of the major ways that Amazon makes its money is through its Web Services division. The division did so well that when Jeff Bezos stepped down as CEO, the head of Amazon Web Services was named the new CEO.78

Stay Focused

The old saying "Rome wasn't built in a day" applies here. Just because you open a business doesn't mean you're going to immediately start making money. It takes time to let people know who you are, so stay focused on achieving your short-term goals.

Many small business owners don't even see a profit for a few years while they use their revenues to recoup investment costs. This is called being "in the red." When you are profitable and make more than you need to spend to cover debts and payroll, this is called being "in the black."

That being said, if the business is not turning a profit after a substantial period of time, it's worth looking into whether there are issues with the product or service, if the market still exists, and other possible issues that might slow or halt a business's growth.

Prepare to Make Sacrifices

The lead-up to starting a business is hard work, but after you open your doors, your work has just begun. In many cases, you have to put in more time than you would if you were working for someone else, which may mean spending less time with family and friends to be successful.

The adage that there are no weekends and no vacations for business owners might ring true for those who are committed to making their business work. There is nothing wrong with full-time employment, and some business owners underestimate the true cost of the sacrifices that are required to start and maintain a profitable business.

Provide Great Service

There are many businesses that forget that providing great customer service is important. If you provide better service for your customers, they'll be more inclined to come to you the next time they need something instead of going to your competition.

In today's hyper-competitive business environment, often the differentiating factor between successful and unsuccessful businesses is the level of service that the business provides. This is where the saying "undersell and overdeliver" comes in, and savvy business owners would be wise to follow it.

Be Consistent

Consistency is a key component to making money in business. You have to keep doing what is necessary to be successful, day in and day out. This will create long-term positive habits that will help you make money in the long run.

DAY 10

Negotiation in Business

The term negotiation refers to a strategic discussion intended to resolve an issue in a way that both parties find acceptable. Negotiations involve give and take, which means one or both parties will usually need to make some concessions.

Negotiation is a strategic discussion between two parties to resolve an issue in a way that both find acceptable. Negotiations can take place between buyers and sellers, employers and prospective employees, or the governments of two or more countries, among others. Successful negotiation usually involves compromises on the part of one or all parties.

Here is everyday simple example of negotiation:

Say you plan to buy a new SUV but don't want to pay the full manufacturer's suggested retail price (MSRP). In that case, you might offer what you consider a fair price. The dealer can accept your offer or counter with another price figure. If you have good negotiating skills, you may be able to drive the price down to a level where you're happy and the dealer is still able to walk away with a profit, albeit a slimmer one.

Another example- Negotiation involving salary negotiations:

For example, you might realize that you are equally willing to accept any of these employment packages: $80,000 per year with two weeks' vacation and 30% travel, $75,000 per year with three weeks' vacation and 25% travel, or $65,000 per year with four weeks' vacation and 5% travel. By making multiple equivalent simultaneous offers, the theory goes, you appear to be a lot more flexible, collect information about the other side's preferences based on which offer she likes best, and increase the odds of reaching a mutually beneficial negotiated agreement.

Characteristics of Negations

Negotiation is the process of discussing each individual's position on a topic and attempting to reach a solution that benefits both parties. All negotiations share four common characteristics:

- The parties involved are somehow interdependent
- The parties are each looking to achieve the best possible result in the interaction for themselves
- The parties are motivated and capable of influencing one another
- The parties believe they can reach an agreement

If these conditions don't exist, neither can a negotiation. The parties have to be interdependent—whether they are experiencing a conflict at work or want to do business with one another. Each has an interest in achieving the best possible result. The parties are motivated and capable of influencing one another, like a union bargaining for better working conditions. A worker doesn't have influence over a manufacturer, but a union of workers does, and without that influence as a factor, both parties won't be motivated to come to the table for discussions. Finally, the parties need to believe they can reach an agreement; otherwise, any negotiation talks will be futile.

There are two basic types of negotiation—distributive and integrative:

Distributive Negotiation:

Distributive negotiation operates under zero-sum conditions. Anything one party gains in the deal is lost by the other party. There can be a winner and a loser, and parties are usually opposing each other. Any relationship between the two parties is usually short term, as at least one party will walk away a "loser" of sorts and animosities can build.

Integrated Negotiation:

Integrated negotiation features a variable number of resources to be divided. In integrated negotiations, both parties can walk away winners. Their primary interests don't make them "opposing parties," but rather they're convergent or congruent with one another. In integrated negotiations, the relationship can be of longer term, because feelings are preserved and no one walks away a loser.

Negotiations involve two or more parties who come together to reach some end goal that is agreeable to all those involved. One party will put its position forward, while the other will either accept the conditions presented or counter with its own position. The process continues until both parties agree to a resolution or negotiations break off without one.

Experienced negotiators will often try to learn as much as possible about the other party's position before a negotiation begins, including what the strengths and weaknesses of that position are, how to prepare to defend their positions, and any counter-arguments the other party will likely make.

The length of time it takes for negotiations to conclude depends on the circumstances. Negotiation can take as little as a few minutes, or, in more complex cases, much longer. For example, a buyer and seller may negotiate for minutes or hours for the sale of a car. But the governments of two or more countries may take months or years to negotiate the terms of a major trade deal.

The Stages of the Negotiation Process

Negotiating can take place between individuals, businesses, governments, and in any other situation where two parties have competing interests. People are intimidated by the negotiation process, and the reason for it is because they think negotiation is personal issue. But negotiation is about solving problems and arriving at win-win solutions for all the parties involved.

Regardless of what you're negotiating over or with whom, negotiation, in simplified terms, is a five-step process.

Step-1. Preparation and Planning

In the preparation and planning stage, you (as a party in the negotiation) need to determine and clarify your own goals in the negotiation. This is a time when you take a moment to define and truly understand the terms and conditions of the exchange and the nature of the conflict. What do you want to walk away with?

You should also take this moment to anticipate the same for the other party. What are their goals in this negotiation? What will they ask for? Do they have any hidden agendas that may come as a surprise to you? What might they settle for, and how does that differ from the outcome you're hoping for? This is a time to develop a strategy for the negotiation.

Before negotiations begin, there are a few questions it helps to ask yourself. Those include:

What do you hope to gain, ideally?

What are your realistic expectations?

What compromises are you willing to make?

What happens if you don'

Preparation can also include finding out as much as you can about the other party and their likely point of view. In the case of the SUV negotiation above, you could probably find out how much room the dealer has to bargain by looking up actual sales prices for that vehicle online.

Also, marshal any facts that will help you make a persuasive case. If you're negotiating for a new job or a raise at work, for instance, come armed with concrete examples of your accomplishments, including hard numbers if possible. Consider bringing testimonials from satisfied clients and/or coworkers if that will buttress your case.

Step-2. Definition of Ground Rules

After the planning and strategy development stage is complete, it's time to work with the other party to define the ground rules and procedures for the negotiation. This is the time when you and the other party will come to agreement on questions like

Who will do the negotiating—will we do it personally or invite a third party?

Where will the negotiation take place?

Will there be time constraints placed on this negotiation process?

Will there be any limits to the negotiation?

If an agreement can't be reached, will there be any specific process to handle that?

Usually, it's during this phase that the parties exchange their initial position. This is the point at which both sides will present their initial positions in terms of what they want and are willing to give in return. Being able to clearly articulate your wishes is critical to the negotiation process. You may not get everything on your wish list, but the other party, if they want to reach a deal, will have a better idea of what it might take to make that happen. You will have a better idea of their position, and where they might be willing to bend, as well.

Step-3. Clarification and Justification

Once initial positions have been exchanged, the clarification and justification stage can begin. Both you and the other party will explain, clarify, bolster and justify your original position or demands. For you, this is an opportunity to educate the other side on your position, and gain further understanding about the other party and how they feel about their side. You might each take the opportunity to explain how you arrived at your current position, and include any supporting documentation. Each party might take this opportunity to review the strategy they planned for the negotiation to determine if it's still an appropriate approach.

This doesn't need to be—and should not be—confrontational, though in some negotiations that's hard to avoid. But if tempers are high moving into this portion of the negotiation process, then those emotions will start to come to a head here. It's important for you to manage those emotions so serious bargaining can begin.

Step-4. Bargaining and Problem Solving

Now that both parties have laid out their case, you're ready to start bargaining. This is the essence of the negotiation process, where the give and take begins. You and the other party will use various negotiation strategies to achieve the goals established during the preparation and planning process. You will use all the information you gathered during the preparation and planning process to present your argument and strengthen your position, or even change your position if the other party's argument is sound and makes sense.

The communication skills of active listening and feedback serve the parties of a negotiation well. It's also important to stick to the issues and allow for an objective discussion to occur. Emotions should be kept under control. Eventually, both parties should agree.

An important key to this step is to hear the other party out and refrain from being dismissive or argumentative. Successful negotiating involves a little give and take on both sides, and an adversarial relationship is likely to be less effective than a collegial one. Also bear in mind that a negotiation can take time, so try not to rush the process or allow yourself to be rushed.

Step-5. Closure and Implementation

Once both parties are satisfied with the results, it's time to end the negotiations. The next step may be in the form of a verbal agreement or a written contract. The latter is usually a better idea as it clearly outlines the position of each party and can be enforced if one party doesn't live up to their end of the bargain.

Once an agreement has been met, this is the stage in which procedures need to be developed to implement and monitor the terms of the agreement. They put all of the information into a format that's acceptable to both parties, and they formalize it. Formalizing the agreement can mean everything from a handshake to a written contract.

Tips for Successful Negotiating

At its most basic, business negotiations are negotiations between corporate entities, their vendors, or their employees. But there is a lot beyond that. In most of our business negotiations, we try to drive a hard bargain, giving away not a penny more than is necessary even as we strive to ensure that our counterpart is satisfied with their outcome. However, figuring out who should get what is rarely easy, but creative solutions to problems in negotiation do exist.

For example, it's not uncommon in business negotiations to find yourself on the brink of an impasse. You and your counterpart have exchanged a series of offers and counteroffers, and you've met somewhere close to the middle—but not close enough. With each side firmly rooted in its position, there may seem to be no way forward. That's when it helps to know how to use MESOs in negotiations. Victoria Husted Medvec and Adam D. Galinsky of Northwestern University argued that, in negotiations involving many issues, you can create a great deal of value by making multiple equivalent simultaneous offers, or MESOs. This negotiation strategy entails identifying several proposals that you value equally and presenting them to the other side.

Research has also shed light on an important aspect of integrative bargaining strategies and business negotiations – namely, the idea of negotiation ethics and fairness when negotiating. In most negotiations, there are three fairness norms that negotiators frequently invoke: equality (an equal split of the resources), equity (a split in proportion to input), and need (a split that favours the negotiator who could most benefit from the resources). Approaching business negotiations with a creative mindset will not only preserve a relationship but also add significant value for both sides creating win-win solutions.

Some people may be born negotiators, but many of us are not. What Makes a Good Negotiator? Some of the key skills of a good negotiator are the ability to listen, to think under pressure, to clearly articulate their point of view, and to be willing to compromise, within reason.

Negotiation Skills

Negotiation skills are highly valuable in the business world, and here we're going to talk about techniques that bring about successful issue resolution. Effective business negotiation is a core leadership and management skill. This is the ability to negotiate effectively in a wide range of business contexts, including dealmaking, employment discussions, corporate team building, labour/management talks, contracts, handling disputes, employee compensation, business acquisitions, vendor pricing and sales, real estate leases, and the fulfilment of contract obligations. Business negotiation is critical to be creative in any negotiation in a business setting. Business negotiation strategies include breaking the problem into smaller parts, considering unusual deal terms, and having your side brainstorm new ideas.

Negotiation is a deliberative process between two or more actors that seek a solution to a common issue or who are bartering over an item of value. Negotiation skills include the range of negotiation techniques negotiators employ to create value and claim value in their dealmaking business negotiations and beyond. Negotiation skills can help you make deals, solve problems, manage conflicts, and build relationships as well as preserve relationships. Negotiation skills can be learned with conscious effort and should be practiced once learned.

Which Negotiating Style Is Best? Is one negotiating style "better" than another? Most research suggests that negotiators with a primarily cooperative style are more successful than hard bargainers at reaching novel solutions that improve everyone's outcomes. Negotiators who lean toward cooperation also tend to be more satisfied with the process and their results, according to Weingart.

Negotiation example: Suppose you're a supplier of a state-of-the-art component for a new medical imaging device. You submit a written sales proposal to the manufacturer. At your initial meeting with the buyer's rep, she asserts: "Your proposal doesn't give us the assurances we need that you can ramp up production if demand skyrockets. Frankly, your price per unit is unacceptable. We think you have a terrific product, but if you're not going to work with us, we're prepared to find someone who will."

Deceptive tactics in negotiation can run rampant: parties "stretch" the numbers, conceal key information, and make promises they know they can't keep. The benefits of negotiation in business offer strong incentives to detect these behaviours. Unfortunately, however, most of us are very poor lie detectors.

Tips for Negotiation Skills

Active Listening.

It is a must for a Win-Win Negotiation. What negotiation skills lead to optimal negotiated agreements and are suitable for win-win negotiations? One skill to cultivate that will have a positive impact on your future negotiation style is active listening. Few negotiators would argue the value of good listening skills. Skilful active listening can calm tensions, break the impasse, and get you the information you need to build creative deals. Yet most people overestimate their ability to deploy this key negotiation skill, while also lacking an accurate understanding of the concept of active listening. Being an active listener is one of the negotiation skills that will help you build creative deals.

Rather, active listening is a dynamic process that can be broken down into three different behaviours: paraphrasing, inquiry, and acknowledgement.

Paraphrase: "It sounds as if you're satisfied with our component overall. But if I understand correctly, you need me to assure you that we can increase production if large orders come in. You're also concerned about our proposed per-unit price and our willingness to work with you to create an acceptable arrangement. Have I captured your main points?"

Inquire: "You mentioned that you found our proposed price to be unacceptable. Help me understand how you came to this conclusion. Let's also talk about how we might set up a pricing structure that you find more reasonable."

Acknowledge: "It sounds as if you're quite disappointed with various elements of our proposal, so much so that you have serious concerns about whether we'll be able to work together over the long haul."

The skilful negotiator orchestrates these aspects of active listening to draw out the other party's concerns and feelings, assert his viewpoint and engage in joint problem-solving.

Justify your Position.

Don't just walk into negotiations without being able to back up your position. Bring information to show that you've done your research and you're committed to reaching a deal.

Put Yourself in their shoes.

Remember that the other side has things it wants out of the deal, too. What can you offer that will help them reach their goal (or most of it) without giving away more than you want to or can afford to?

Keep your emotions in check.

It's easy to get caught up in the moment and be swayed by your personal feelings, especially ones like anger and frustration. But don't let your emotions cause you to lose sight of your goal.

Know when to walk away.

Before you begin the negotiating process, it's a good idea to know what you'll accept as a bare minimum and when you'd rather walk away from the table than continue to bargain. There is no use trying to reach a deal if both sides are hopelessly dug in. Even if you don't want to end negotiations entirely, pausing them can give everyone involved a chance to regroup and possibly return to the table with a fresh perspective.

Understanding Zone Of Possible Agreement (ZOPA)

ZOPA is an acronym from the business world. It stands for the zone of possible agreement. ZOPA is a way of visualizing where the positions of the parties to a negotiation overlap. It is within that zone that compromises can be reached. Not a physical place, the zone of possible agreement or bargaining range is considered an area where two or more negotiating parties may find common ground. It is this area where parties will often compromise and strike a deal.

For negotiating parties to find a settlement or reach an agreement, they must work towards a common goal and seek an area that incorporates at least some of each party's ideas.

A zone of possible agreement (ZOPA) is a bargaining range in an area where two or more negotiating parties may find common ground. A ZOPA can only exist when there is some overlap between each party's expectations regarding an agreement. If negotiating parties cannot reach a ZOPA, they are in a negative bargaining zone.

No matter how much negotiation occurs, an agreement can never be reached outside of the zone of possible agreement. To reach an agreement successfully, negotiating parties must understand one another's needs, values and interests.

A ZOPA can only exist if there is some overlap between what all parties are willing to accept from a deal. For example, for Tom to sell his car to John for a minimum $5,000, John must be willing to pay at least $5,000. If John is willing to offer $5,500 for the car, then there is an overlap between his and Tom's bottom lines. If John can only offer $4,750 for the car, then there is no overlap, and there cannot be a ZOPA.

Negative Bargaining Zones. When negotiating parties cannot reach a ZOPA, they are in a negative bargaining zone. A deal cannot be reached in a negative bargaining zone, as the needs and desires of all parties cannot be met by a deal made under such circumstances. For example, let's say that Dave wants to sell his mountain bike and gear for $700 to buy new skis and ski gear. Suzy wants to buy the bike and gear for $400, and can't go any higher. Dave and Suzy have not reached a ZOPA; they are in a negative bargaining zone.

However, negative bargaining zones can be overcome if negotiating parties are willing to learn about one another's desires and needs. For example, let's say Dave explains to Suzy that he wants to use the proceeds from the sale of the bike to buy new skis and ski gear. Suzy has a pair of gently-used, high-quality skis that she is willing to part with. Dave is willing to take less cash for the mountain bike if Suzy throws the used skis in. The two parties have reached a ZOPA and can, therefore, make a successful deal.

DAY 11

Organizational Leadership

In Every company, strong leaders are always needed. If you can demonstrate your ability as a leader and a preference for leadership responsibilities as an employee, you will most likely be allowed to head a team or project. Learning more about business leadership and what it takes to be a good leader will help the company to become a more valued asset in any workplace.

Traditionally, leadership is thought of as a set of outward-facing capabilities that allow you to bring out the best in colleagues, along with an inward self-awareness to appreciate your impact on others.

Organizational leadership is slightly more nuanced than team leadership, as it refers to the skills and qualities needed to run an entire division, department, or company. While the broader understanding of leadership focuses more on interpersonal skills needed to organize team members around a common goal, successful organizational leadership requires a certain level of business acumen. In other words, those aspiring to organizational leadership roles must deliver traditional leadership skills at scale.

Organizational leadership is the ability to lead groups of individuals toward fulfilling an organization's mission. It encompasses the following skills:

Understanding an organization's mission, in alignment with one's strengths.
Creating a strategic plan in line with that mission.
Implementing goals and holding teams accountable for accomplishing those goals within an established timeline, and in alignment with the strategic plan.

Foreseeing possible challenges in the road ahead.

Innovating to meet those challenges.

Pivoting effectively as circumstances change.

Remaining calm amidst uncertainty.

Communicating effectively.

Inspiring groups of individuals to do their best and work toward a unified purpose.

Addressing the concerns of internal stakeholders and the community at large.

Doing all of the above, with an eye on inclusivity, integrity, and authenticity.

The above skills are predicated on the leader's expertise, learned managerial skills, growth mindset, and developed emotional intelligence. They allow the leader to be aware of oneself, their impact on others, and the motivation of others, within the context of furthering the organization's singular mission.

Why is organizational leadership important?

Traditional management has been downplayed in recent years as "maintaining" the status quo. With innovation and disruption happening at record speed, management doing things as they've always been done is not enough. Organizational leadership is needed at every level to consider how current practices can be further improved or changed to meet future needs.

Effective leaders are required in all successful organisations and businesses. Effective and well-trained leadership is critical to achieving an agreed-upon aim for the company's success. When it comes to forming and expressing new strategic directions, as well as engaging with and encouraging people to enhance their commitment to corporate goals, leaders are crucial.

Leaders must be adaptable and adaptive in this continuously evolving market, where a global focus, digital requirements, and social-political developments are all frequent. Being able to recover fast and in a constantly changing corporate environment, staying the course in the face of recurring challenges is important.

Any successful company leader understands the importance of delegating. This should result in the development of future business leaders.

Leaders must wear numerous hats to lead their organisations. An effective leader instils passion in his or her personnel while also bringing out the best in them. In addition, employees should feel protected and supported in their working environment.

Organizational leadership is important because it:

Motivates team members. Team members respond in kind to the leader. They will be motivated to mirror the growth mindset for their teams and themselves and consider how they can personally contribute to the forward momentum of the organization as a whole.

Allows for a problem-solving and decision-making mindset. In a psychologically safe atmosphere where people are not afraid to speak up, great ideas can emerge. When a leader entrusts the individuals hired into their roles to develop solutions and make decisions, exponential growth is possible.

Promotes communication, ethics, inclusion, and respect. The highly emotionally intelligent organizational leader communicates in all ways that all employee's contributions are respected, as every role is vital to the organization's forward movement as a whole. The leader shares the organization's values and models the communication, ethics, inclusion, and respect expected of each individual.

Allows organizational leaders to remain goal-oriented. With individuals empowered to fulfil their roles and develop innovative solutions, the organizational leader may focus on the larger picture: moving the mission forward with an eye on navigating the challenges ahead.

Who Needs Organizational Leadership Skills?

All professionals—no matter their position—need leadership skills to succeed in their careers. Yet, organizational leadership skills are particularly important for the following:

Aspiring executives: Successfully running a division, department, or entire organization requires specific leadership skills. As an aspiring executive, you need to know how to execute the strategy guiding your organization.

Experienced team leaders: If you already have experience leading a team, developing your organizational leadership skills is the next step toward applying your knowledge at scale.

Entrepreneurs: As an entrepreneur, your leadership skills are an integral component of your business's success. You need a strong foundation in organizational leadership to build your business from the ground up and adapt to change as the company grows and faces new challenges.

Early and mid-career professionals: Developing leadership skills early in your career can allow you to demonstrate leadership potential and be positioned for a promotion into a more senior role.

Newly appointed leaders: If you've primarily worked as an independent contributor but now find yourself in leadership roles, developing your skills can enable you to perform your duties more effectively.

New or aspiring entrepreneurs: Entrepreneurs are, by default, the leaders of their venture. Your startup's success requires you to get as much value as possible from your team to free yourself up for critical strategic work.

Organizational Leadership Skills and Qualities

1. An Understanding of Your Business

To lead your organization to success, you need a clear understanding of its inner workings, as well as the context in which it operates. This includes external forces, such as industry trends and changes in consumer behaviour and preferences.

It's also important to look inward to understand your organization's structure and dynamics. If a misalignment exists between the internal and external forces shaping the business, it can be detrimental to its success.

Using your analysis of those internal and external forces, you need to develop a vision for your division, unit, or company and inspire those around you to execute on it. This requires communication with every level of your organization and leading through other managers. This is particularly challenging in contexts with dispersed teams and multi-site operations—especially in an age defined by remote work.

2. Communication and Interpersonal Skills

Strong communication and interpersonal skills are essential to organizational leadership. Other interpersonal skills, like emotional intelligence, active listening, and delegation, are also necessary to organize your team around common goals. You must be able to shape your organization's architecture to execute on your vision, which requires aligning its people, culture, and systems to deliver on tasks that create value and help your company grow.

3. Change Management and Innovation

To be a successful organizational leader, you need to manage change effectively. One of your main goals should be to execute your vision and strategy and lead your organization to success. To do so, changes throughout your company will likely need to be made. Unsurprisingly, communication plays an important role in change management. There are, however, many other components that come into play. For example, organization and a keen eye for detail are essential to keeping your strategy on track. Additionally, you need to identify opportunities for positive change, define a strategy to implement that change and garner colleagues' support.

4. Self-awareness and Personal Development

Finally, becoming a strong organizational leader requires self-awareness and a commitment to continuous personal development. If you want to become a better leader, conducting a self-assessment of your strengths and weaknesses is a great starting point. To do so, pay attention to your leadership style, and don't be afraid to ask for feedback from colleagues. After you've identified your strengths and weaknesses, you can devise a plan to hone your skills.

5. Qualities of good leader:

- Integrity
- Ability to delegate
- Communication

- Self-awareness
- Gratitude
- Learning agility
- Influence
- Empathy
- Courage
- Respect

What Are the Top Leadership Skills for Business?

1. Emotional Intelligence

Emotional intelligence is an individual's ability to recognize and manage emotions in themselves and others. It's typically broken into four areas:

Self-awareness: The ability to recognize your own strengths, weaknesses, and emotions.

Self-management: The ability to regulate your emotions, especially during periods of high stress.

Social awareness: The ability to recognize others' emotions. This is also often referred to as the ability to exhibit empathy.

Relationship management: The ability to manage relationships with others through influencing, coaching, mentoring, and resolving conflict.

Emotional intelligence is a critical skill for all leaders. It's so important that it influences most of the remaining skills in this list. By developing your emotional intelligence, you can better communicate, motivate your team, delegate tasks, and remain flexible under pressure—in short, the requirements of being an effective leader.

2. Communication

A leader's communication abilities are critical to a team's success. To understand why, you need to think about the role leaders fill: They motivate others to follow them and work toward shared goals.

The ability to effectively communicate with others also affects the efficiency of the group and determines how tasks are accomplished. To ensure these tasks are done correctly, you must determine if you're exhibiting the effective communication skills required to inform your team of your goals and plan to achieve them.

Communication is made up of several discrete skills. Some of the most important communication skills for leaders include:

Adaptability: The ability to adapt your communication style to different situations and audiences.

Active listening: The ability to remain engaged and attentive during conversation, paying attention to verbal and non-verbal forms of communication.

Transparency: The ability to communicate your company's goals, opportunities, challenges, and strategy in an open and transparent way.

Clarity: The ability to simplify a message by providing the right level of detail for a given audience to motivate them to act.

Inquisitiveness: The ability to ask open-ended questions that spark thoughtful discussion.

Empathy: As mentioned above, the ability to recognize the emotions of those you communicate with and using that understanding to adjust your communication style.

Body language: Presenting open and comforting body language that builds rapport and makes others feel comfortable sharing opinions.

3. The Ability to Bring Out the Best Performance

An effective leader doesn't simply tell others what to do or micromanage how tasks are completed. Instead, they empower employees to do what they were hired for. This not only improves team performance but frees up time to perform essential leadership tasks, which can greatly improve time management. All of these elements affect overall team performance—a clear indicator of whether you demonstrate effective leadership.

How you choose to empower your employees depends on several factors, including the type of work being done and the goals you're working toward. There's a wide range of strategies you can use as a leader, including:

- Building a culture of trust in your organization
- Delivering honest feedback
- Showing empathy
- Fostering open communication
- Being purpose-driven
- Supporting growth opportunities

As a bonus, research has shown that organizations with highly empowered employees enjoy additional benefits, such as greater job satisfaction, which leads to lower levels of turnover and higher levels of engagement.

4. Self-Awareness

To capably lead your team, it's important to have a healthy level of self-awareness. This can allow you to recognize and control your emotions as you perform your duties, helping you remain effective during particularly stressful situations.

Additionally, self-awareness is one of the most essential leadership qualities because it can empower you to identify your leadership style.

5. Resilience

In business, things rarely go exactly as intended. No matter how well your account for known risks in your business strategy or product launch, there will always be variables that can throw a wrench in your plans. As a leader, you must remain flexible and resilient under pressure and possess critical problem-solving skills that will help you adjust to changing scenarios and guide your team to new courses of action.

There are many ways to build resilience in your leadership style. Some effective strategies include:

Reflecting on a situation and assessing options before acting

Striving to continuously learn and improve yourself and your team

Remaining purpose-driven at all times, even during stressful situations

Cultivating strong relationships with friends, colleagues, and mentors you can leverage during times of crisis

6. Financial Literacy

Finally, it's important to recognize that much of a leader's time is dedicated to business strategy: selecting organizational goals and striving to reach them. By necessity, these goals will largely be tied to questions of financial performance: profitability, cash flow, and other key metrics. With this in mind, all business leaders should maintain financial literacy.

In addition to basic financial literacy, financial skills all leaders need include:

Financial statement analysis, which encompasses balance sheets, income statements, and cash flow statements.

Ratio analysis, which allows for a more meaningful understanding of a company's performance.

Cash flow management is crucial to keeping a business running and growing at a consistent rate.

Forecasting refers to the ability to predict future sales, cash flows, and profits.

What Are the Different Leadership Styles?

Approachability: A leadership style embodied by warmth and authenticity that builds deep connections with team members.

Credibility: A leadership style embodied by humility, competence, and resolve, in which the team views the leader as deserving of their trust and commitment.

Aspiration: A leadership style embodied by a clear vision and high expectations, which motivates team members to perform to their fullest potential.

Once you understand the leadership style you default to, you can leverage its strengths while avoiding its potential pitfalls. You can also be positioned to develop a unique leadership style.

As with several of the other skills in this list, your ability to be self-aware ties back to emotional intelligence.

Organisational Leadership Skills

Leadership skills are essential for any professional who wants to advance their career and make a positive impact in their organization. Organizational leadership skills are the skills used to inspire individuals to achieve their goals and support the organization's strategic goals. Organizational leadership affects the performance and success of an organization. It's important to have strong organizational leadership skills so you're able to lead others effectively to generate excellent results for your company and support it in achieving its goals. Leaders often create an example for others through their behaviour, so demonstrating excellent skills may provide employees with good direction for modelling their behaviour. As a result, this creates a stronger, more productive company culture.

While exact skills may vary for each person, industry and organization, some examples of these skills include:

Ability to influence others: Leaders need to understand how to persuade and influence others. This helps them identify what motivates a specific person and leverage this knowledge to develop trust and inspire them to succeed.

Communication: Communication skills empower leaders to share critical information, learn more about their peers and develop good relationships. It may be beneficial for leaders to be extroverts.

Delegation: Leaders must avoid keeping all work for themselves and micromanaging others. Excellent leaders understand how to delegate work to others, especially giving tasks to people based on what they enjoy and succeed with the most.

Emotional intelligence: Emotional intelligence helps professionals understand each other and process their own emotions. Leaders may experience a range of challenges during their careers, so they must be able to regulate their emotions and respond appropriately.

Practicality: While it's beneficial for leaders to be creative and innovative, it's also important for them to be practical, especially when developing solutions for problems. Organizational leaders often focus on facts to think critically and determine the best evidence-based decisions.

Problem-solving: Problem-solving skills enable leaders to evaluate their options and determine the best solution. This requires performing research, discerning the most beneficial outcomes and choosing the appropriate way to resolve a concern.

Self-control: Although it's essential for organizational leaders to maintain a proactive approach to their work, they also understand the importance of pausing, listening and thinking about their tasks. Self-control may also assist with stress management, which may benefit the entire time.

How To Improve Organizational Leadership Skills

Organizational leadership is a leadership method related to establishing strategic goals for an organization. It also involves inspiring an organization's employees to pursue and achieve their own goals to support the organization and its strategic objectives. Demonstrating organizational leadership requires a specific skill set that may be beneficial for many professionals to develop to become more effective in their roles. In this article, we define what organizational leadership skills are, explain why they're important, outline how to improve them and offer tips for practising them.

Lead yourself: leadership starts with you, to be a great leader you must be able to lead yourself. Can you? For example, can you: Plan? And review?

Leadership is situational. So, leadership starts with mindset. It continues as you develop the ability to lead yourself. Then, as you move your focus to the leadership of others, you must realise that it is situational. Ken Blanchard was probably the first to fully articulate this point, that essentially the leadership of others depends on responding appropriately to the combination of their current competence and their current motivation. For example, if someone is highly motivated and highly competent you can simply leave them to it after the correct briefing; this is known as delegation. If someone is new to the job or role and thus not very competent, yet, but is also highly motivated, then they simply need direction. Good leaders recognise that their default style is not perfect for all situations and constantly adjust it as the occasion demands. lead yourself. Then, as you move your focus to the leadership of others.

Follow these steps to improve your organizational leadership skills:

1. Evaluate your skills

Begin your skill-building process by evaluating your current abilities. Think about your abilities and natural tendencies, and consider completing assessments that provide objective results about your skill levels. This may allow you to identify your strengths and weaknesses and understand what to focus on improving.

2. Pursue training

Explore training options to improve your skills. Consider pursuing training to develop specific skills through online courses, seminars or reading materials. Another option for improving your organizational leadership skills may be to seek formal education. Think about earning an advanced degree, such as a master's degree in organizational leadership, to help refine your skills.

3. Practice your skills

Look for opportunities to develop and practice your skills both personally and professionally. If you pursue a degree to help you develop your skills, consider participating in experiential learning. This learning method allows you to apply your skills to practical scenarios, helping you prepare to handle situations within your organization.

Develop a personal leadership philosophy

A personal leadership philosophy is a set of principles that you identify with and use to guide your actions and decisions. This may provide you with a framework to apply for setting strategic goals and leading others. To develop your philosophy, think about your expectations, priorities and values, and consider what's important to you.

Be proactive

Maintain a proactive approach to leading your organization. Developing a strategic plan allows you to practice your organizational leadership skills. If a challenge occurs, implementing this strategic plan and remaining calm may help others trust you and your abilities.

Promote community

Create an environment that fosters a sense of community and belonging. Aim to ensure each employee understands and identifies with the organization's strategic goals. This may help improve employee engagement and, as a result, provide benefits to the organization, like lower turnover rates and increased employee satisfaction.

Understand your audience

Organizational leaders need to know the people that they're leading well. Get to know each employee on a personal level and focus on learning about their goals and what motivates them. This may help you improve their productivity and accountability and inspire them to succeed.

Encourage accountability

Organizational leadership combines personal and shared success. Promote accountability among your team to ensure each person feels a sense of responsibility for projects. This may help prevent complications or disagreements among your team. Instead, a culture of accountability may motivate them to focus on finding solutions rather than determining who to blame for the issues.

Ask for feedback

Feedback is an effective way to learn about your performance and possible areas for improvement. Ask the employees you lead and your peers in leadership to provide you with feedback about your performance. Encourage them to be honest about what you do well and what areas you may benefit from improving. Use this feedback to adapt your approach

Know your vision

The first step to developing leadership skills is to have a clear and compelling vision of what you want to achieve and why. Your vision should align with your organization's mission, values, and goals, and reflect your passion and purpose. A strong vision will help you communicate your direction, set priorities, and inspire others to join you.

Build trust and credibility

The second step to developing leadership skills is to establish trust and credibility with your team, peers, and stakeholders. Trust is the foundation of any effective relationship, and credibility is the result of your actions and words. To build trust and credibility, be honest, respectful, consistent, and reliable. Show empathy, listen actively, and give constructive feedback.

Empower and develop others

The third step to developing leadership skills is to empower and develop others. Your role is not to do everything yourself, but to delegate, coach, and mentor your team members. Give them autonomy, responsibility, and support, and help them grow their skills and confidence. Recognize their achievements, celebrate their successes, and encourage their learning.

Foster collaboration and innovation

The fourth step to developing leadership skills is to foster collaboration and innovation. As a leader, you need to create a culture of teamwork, where everyone feels valued, included, and engaged. Promote diversity, creativity, and openness, and encourage your team to share ideas, opinions, and feedback. Facilitate problem-solving, decision-making, and conflict resolution.

Keep learning and improving

The sixth and final step to developing leadership skills is to keep learning and improving. Constantly seek new knowledge, skills, and perspectives, and apply them to your work. Reflect on your strengths and weaknesses, and seek feedback and guidance from others. Embrace change, challenge yourself, and pursue your personal and professional goals.

Here's what else to consider

This is a space to share examples, stories, or insights that don't fit into any of the previous sections. What else would you like to add?

Day12

Advertising

"Advertising is any paid form of non-personal communication of ideas, goods and service by an identified sponsor." -Philip Kottler

"Advertising is a means of communication with the users of a product or service. Advertisements are messages paid for by those who send them and are intended to inform or influence people who receive them," -Advertising Association of the UK

Advertising is the concept of communicating a message about products and services to a customer so that the customer can understand the offering along with its features, uniqueness, price, offer, benefits and value to get convinced about making a purchase. Advertising is done using various media like TV, print, radio, online, digital, social media, outdoor and more where advertisements are showcased showing the value to the customer. It is one of the most critical components of Example of Advertising

One of the great examples of effective advertising can be the Apple's campaign of 1984 which was based on the theme of 'Think Different' and was launched during the Super Bowl along with other channels. It is a very famous campaign which established Apple as personal computer company and launched Macintosh as a ground breaking product. It represented the Apple brand for many years It had a message which connected to the audience along with the theme. Also, the execution of the creative idea was done quite well. marketing.

In corporate world, advertising plays a very significant role, it is used to build brand image. When we introduce any product or services in the market then advertising is the most important tool to aware the consumer about our product. With the help of advertising, we reach our product or services directly to the end-users and also increase our sales by the advertising. Advertising industry is made by group of companies which advertise agencies that create the advertisements for product and services.

Several companies are producing goods and products, which are critical for a customer to fulfil their needs. However, with tremendous competition and limited span of attention for a customer, it becomes difficult for a customer to know about a product or a service. Companies also have a limited & stagnated market share.

When we developed the new product consumers need *information about product and services*. Information given in an advertisement may be about the company and its product or services. Brand image building Image is the mental picture of brand that may appeal to their target audience in varying degrees. Images projected are geared to match the need and expectations of the end customers.

Product innovation is a very challenging task and advertising perform this task most effectively for new products but it must be pointed that advertising does not guarantee the success of all new products.

New product launch refers to modification in existing product or developing of new product, imitation of competitive product and product line acquisitions. Advertising used to promote new products and reflect the image in the minds of target audience. Acceptance of advertising increases the potential for *raising revenues*.

Role of Advertising in Marketing Mix

Advertising plays a very important role in marketing mix; it is all pervasive facet of most growing communities. Advertising has important consequences for the advertisers who use it and or individuals also who are exposed it. Advertising is the element of promotion it is not only used in promoting the product, but also affects the following variables of marketing mix.

Communication with consumer

Persuasion

Contribution to Economic Growth

Catalyst for change

Communication with Consumers:

Advertising is a major source of communication between manufacturer and other companies which providing services or put ideas and concepts at one hand and on the other hand customers, buyers. Advertising reminding the product to the existing customers and aim to developed new prospects. Advertising refers as effective communication with the target audience.

Persuasion:

Advertising used to persuade the prospective buyers or customers to buy a product and services. Success of all business industries depends upon the planned and effective persuasion. Consumer should be aware about advertiser's persuasive interest where no matter that how informative the message may be which convey in the advertisement.

Contribution to Economic Growth

Advertising contributes in economic growth by expand the market for new product and services and helps to develop also new market segment.

Catalyst for Change:

Two aspects of special significance are the originality of the message communicated and the second one is the eventual effect on the consumer's standard of living. The ability to change comes from originality, ingenuity, innovation and imagination in advertising. It can help in promoting new products and ideas as well as upgrading products and brands used by existing consumers. The main contribution of advertising is to bring about change especially relevant to developing countries.

An effective advertising campaign can help you to:

increase customer reach.

build customer awareness of your business and brand.

promote the benefits of your products or services.

communicate information about your business.

increase sales and demand.

gain an advantage over your competitors.

Objectives of Advertising

The prime objectives of advertising is to promote the goods and services in the market. It contains:

Tell the market about the new product

To suggest the new uses for a product

To inform the market about the price change

Explain the target customer that, how the product works

Improving the brand image of the product

Building a company image building brand preference

Encouraging people to switch their brand

To change the customer's perception about product attributes

To persuade the customer for purchasing now.

To remind the consumer from where they buy the product.

Advantages of Advertising

There are certain benefits of advertising. Some advantages are:

1. It helps marketers to reach out to make people by creating awareness.

2. It promotes the value and utility of the brand to customers

3. Good advertisements help build a strong community and induce brand loyalty

4. Companies who focus on advertising are also perceived as big brands, which pushes customers to believe that products and services are also good

5. Creative teams form advertising agencies give good inputs about a brand by creating more brand awareness.

6. Helps sales force, retailers, shop owners to promote the products in a much better way

7. It helps build trust between customers, retailers, suppliers and manufacturers

Components of Advertising

Advertising can be broadly broken down into four major components:

1. Strategy

Focuses on the message, customer segment to be targeted, integrated marketing communication (IMC) channels and the budget which is core of the advertising campaign. The overall product strategy should be aligned with the advertising messaging and channels.

2. Media

Choosing the most appropriate channel, medium or media to reach out to the customers is very important based on the target audience demographics and other attributes. Reaching customers on a channel where they are not present will not benefit them at all.

3. Creative idea

This is the message, theme or visual which can be made to attract the customer. Sometimes straightforward information advertising can work but many times they need to be creative and should have a theme around which the entire messaging is based.

4. Creative Execution

The final advertisement was created based on the creative idea. Without proper execution of the strategy, media and the idea, the campaign would not be able to fulfil its purpose and it will lead to losses. The execution needs to be done in a planned manner so that the idea is presented well to the customer.

Types of Advertising Media

It is a massive exercise for any company. There are many options where ads can be showcased through an advertising medium. Companies often use all the media available to do a 360-degree branding. Some different types of media used by companies are mentioned below:

1. TV

Television is one of the most developed ways to advertise. Advertising on TV is an effective way to reach to millions of people, as TVs have an extremely high penetration worldwide. The ad slots are given by broadcasting companies. Higher TRP and GRP programs help reach out to wider audience.

2. Radio

Radio channels offer ad slots to companies who can communicate their message to the customers.

3. Print

This type of media includes magazines, newspapers, brochures etc. which can be used to advertise about the products and services offered by a company. This has been the most widely used media till date.

4. Online

With the growth in internet penetration, companies often use digital media with online advertising to reach out to customer using social media, browsing websites etc. It also includes content marketing, blogging, viral marketing etc.

5. Outdoor

Using hoardings, standees, OOH (out of home) media are covered under outdoor advertising. This enables companies to reach out to those who are not an home but are outside their homes or office during transit.

6. Mobile

Use of services like SMS and social media groups has also made mobile an effective tool for advertising.

Advertising Strategies

There are Push & Pull are the types of strategies that advertising managers follow:

Push Strategy

The ultimate aim of the push strategy is to convince retailers, wholesalers, salespersons, or dealers to carry and sell the advertiser's product. Companies push their products to them by offering inducements, such as providing advertising kits to help the retailer sell the product, wholesalers for bulk selling offering incentives to carry stock, and developing trade promotions.

Pull Strategy

The ultimate aim of the pull strategy is to convince the target audience that they try, make purchases and repurchase the product. In this process companies pull their product directly appealing to the target consumer with coupons, in-store displays, and sweepstakes.

Budgeting for Advertising

When the advertising objective has been selected, then the companies must focus on the advertising budget. Budgeting can be a difficult process because brand managers need a large resource allocation to promote their product and services in the market. Before preparing the budget, companies must take into consideration the various factors such as advertising frequency, competition, market share, and product life cycle stage and product differentiation.

There are various methods which are used to developing advertising budgets are as follows:

1. Percentage of Sales Method

This is the most common method used by small businesses because it's so simple. For using this method, advertisers take a percentage of past data or anticipated sales and use this percentage for overall budget for advertising. This method can be effective if the business compares its sales with those of the competition when figuring its budget.

2. Objective and Task Method

This method is mostly used by large businesses. This method allows advertisers that correlate advertising expenditures to overall marketing objectives. This correlation is very important in spending focus on primary business goals. Once the objectives have been established, the advertiser determines how much cost will occur to meet them.

3. Competitive Parity Method

It is used for businesses to compare item advertising expenditure with its competitors. The theory behind this method is that if the business is aware of how much its competitor are spending to inform, persuade and remind about their product and services then the business can remain competitive, spending more or less or same on their own advertising.

4. Market Share Method

In this method, a business market share is equal with its advertising expenditures. This method is also similar with competitive parity method, in which budgeting strategies based on external market trends.

5. Unit Sales Method

In this method, cost of an individual item can multiply by the number of units that advertisers wish to sell.

6. All Available Funds Method

This method involves the allocation of all available profits to advertising purpose. This type of methods is useful when a newly start-up business is trying to increase awareness of its product and services among the consumers.

7. Affordable Methods

In this method, advertisers are making their budget on affordable methods of advertising. What they can afford in advertising is often a complex task, so they need to incorporate overall objectives, competition, sales trends, operating costs etc.

Media Planning

Media planning is the process of determining how much time and space will be used to achieve advertising objectives. There are various media for planning an advertisement and choosing the best media among various media is a complex task which helps to inform and persuade the target consumer. Media planning is about, reaching the right people at the right time with the right message.

Selection of the best media is a challenging task. Selecting the best media vehicle is the essential part of buying which fit the target audience means the time and place where the audience is most receptive to the message. It is the responsibility of the buyer that he chooses the best vehicles.

Price is the important factor in buying nothing is more crucial in media buying than securing the lowest possible price for promotion. Time and space are the two important factors that charge highly in the advertising budget so we negotiate the price as low as possible.

Vehicle performance must be monitored from time to time for a successful campaign. Vehicles that poorly performing must be replaced or costs must be modified because delay in response can affect brand sales.

Post-campaign analysis is very important for expected results. After completing the campaign, the planner should compare the expected plan with the forecast plan and see what happened.

The agency may be contractually obligated to pay the initial invoice, or because of various negotiations between an ad agency and selected media, it can be beneficial for the agency to make payments and then bill the clients. The Media planner is responsible for paying the bills.

Advertising management

Advertising management is a planned managerial process designed to oversee and control the various advertising activities involved in a program to communicate with a firm's target market which is ultimately designed to influence the consumer's purchase decisions.

Simply put, the role of advertising management is to develop and place the ads in the most relevant places that will bring the best results. The scope of ad management includes analysing the current advertising strategy and target audience, evaluating its effectiveness, and updating it toward existing goals.

An example of advertising management is creating an advertising campaign for a new product. This includes creating a budget, developing a creative strategy, selecting media outlets, designing creative materials, placing ads, measuring results, and optimizing the campaign.

Advertising management is a complex process that involves making many-layered decisions including developing advertising strategies, setting an advertising budget, setting advertising objectives, determining the target market, media strategy (which involves media planning), and developing the message strategy.

Advertising simply put is telling and selling the product. Advertising Management though is a complex process of employing various media to sell a product or service. This process begins quite early from the marketing research and encompasses the media campaigns that help sell the product.

Without an effective advertising management process in place, the media campaigns are not that fruitful and the whole marketing process goes for a toss. Hence, companies that believe in an effective advertising management process are always a step ahead in terms of selling their goods and services.

Advertising management begins from the market research phase. At this point, the data produced by marketing research is used to identify what types of advertising would be adequate for the specific product.

Gone are the days when there was only print and television advertising available to the manufacturers. These days apart from print and television, radio, mobile, and Internet are also available as advertising media. The advertising management process helps in defining the outline of the media campaign and in deciding which type of advertising would be used before the launch of the product.

If you wish to make the advertising effective, always remember to include it from the market research time. Market research will help to identify the niche segment of the population to which the product or service has to be targeted from a large population. It will also identify why the niche segment would opt for the product or service. This information will serve as a guideline for the preparation of advertising campaigns.

Once the niche segments are identified and the determination of what types of advertising will be used is done, then the advertising management focuses on creating the specifics for the overall advertising campaign. If it is a radio campaign, which type of ads would be used, if it is a print campaign, what write ups and ads will be used, and if it is a television campaign, what type of commercials will be used?

There might also be a mix-and-match advertising in which radio might supplement television advertising and so on. It is important that through advertising management the image is conveyed that all the strategies complement each other. It should not look to the public that the radio advertising is focusing on something else while television on something else. The whole process in the end should benefit the product or service.

The role of people designing the advertising campaign is crucial to its success. They have been trained by seasoned professionals who provide training in the specific field. Designing an advertising campaign is no small task and understanding consumer behaviour from the data collected from market research is a very important aspect of the campaign.

A whole lot of creativity and inspiration is required to launch an adequate advertising campaign. In addition, management skills come into play when the work has to be done keeping the big picture in mind. It would be fruitful for the company if the advertising campaign lasts well over the lifetime of a product or service, reach the right customers, and generate the desired revenue.

Steps in the process of advertising

Mass demand has been created almost entirely through the development of Advertising. For the development of advertising and to get the best results one needs to follow the advertising process step by step. The following are the steps involved in the process of advertising:

Step 1 - Briefing: The advertiser needs to brief about the product or the service which has to be advertised and do the SWOT analysis of the company and the product.

Step 2 - Knowing the Objective: One should first know the objective or the purpose of advertising. i.e. what message is to be delivered to the audience?

Step 3 - Research: This step involves finding out the market behaviour, knowing the competitors, what type of advertising they are using, what the response of the consumers, availability of the resources needed in the process, etc.

Step 4 - Target Audience: The next step is to identify the target consumers most likely to buy the product. The target should be appropriately identified without any confusion. E.g., if the product is a healthy drink for growing kids, then the target customers will be the parents who are going to buy it and not the kids who are going to drink it.

Step 5 - Media Selection: Now that the target audience is identified, one should select an appropriate media for advertising so that the customers who are to be informed about the product and are willing to buy are successfully reached.

Step 6 - Setting the Budget: Then the advertising budget has to be planned so that there is no shortage of funds or excess of funds during the process of advertising and also there are no losses to the company.

Step 7 - Designing and Creating the Ad: First the design which is the outline of the ad on papers is made by the copywriters of the agency, and then the actual creation of ad is done with help of the art directors and the creative personnel of the agency.

Step 8 - Perfection: Then the created ad is re-examined and the ad is redefined to make it perfect to enter the market.

Step 9 - Place and Time of Ad: The next step is to decide where and when the ad will be shown. The place will be decided according to the target customers where the ad is most visible clearly to them. The finalization of the time on which the ad will be telecasted or shown on the selected media will be done by the traffic department of the agency.

Step 10 - Execution: Finally, the advertisement is released with perfect creation, perfect placement and perfect timing in the market.

Step 11 - Performance: The last step is to judge the performance of the ad in terms of the response from the customers, whether they are satisfied with the ad and the product, did the ad reached all the targeted people, was the advertiser capable enough to compete with the other players, etc. Every point is studied properly and changes are made, if any.

If these steps are followed properly then there has to be a successful beginning for the product in the market.

Advertising Techniques

Today every company needs to advertise its product to inform the customers about the product, increase sales, acquire market value, and gain a reputation and name in the industry. Every business spends a lot of money for advertising their products but the money spent will lead to success only when the best techniques of advertising are used for the product. So here are some very common and most used techniques used by advertisers to get desired results.

Emotional Appeal

This technique of advertising is done with help of two factors - the needs of consumers and the fear factor.

The most common appeals under need are:

Need for something new

Need to get acceptance

Need for not being ignored

Need for change of old things

Need for security

Need to become attractive, etc.

Most common appeals under fear are:

Fear of accident

Fear of death

Fear of being avoided

Fear of getting sick

Fear of getting old, etc.

Promotional Advertising

This technique involves giving away samples of the product for free to the consumers. The items are offered at trade fairs, promotional events, and ad campaigns to gain the attention of the customers.

Bandwagon Advertising

This type of technique involves convincing the customers to join the group of people who have bought this product and be on the winning side. E.g. recent Pantene shampoo ad says "15crores women trusted Pantene, and you?"

Facts and Statistics

Here, advertisers use numbers, proofs, and real examples to show how well their product works. E.g. "Lizol floor cleaner cleans 99.99% germs" or "Colgate is recommended by 70% of the dentists of the world" or Eno - just 6 seconds.

Unfinished Ads

The advertisers here just play with words by saying that their product works better but don't answer how much more than the competitor. E.g., Lays - no one can eat just one or Horlicks - more nutrition daily. The ads don't say who can eat more or how much more nutrition.

Weasel Words

In this technique, the advertisers don't say that they are the best from the rest, but don't also deny it. E.g., Sunsilk Hair fall Solution - reduces hair fall. The ad doesn't say stop hair fall.

Endorsements

Advertisers use celebrities to advertise their products. The celebrities or stars endorse the product by describing their own experiences with the product.

Complementing the Customers

Here, the advertisers used punch lines which complement the consumers who buy their products. E.g. Revlon says "Because you are worth it."

Ideal Family and Ideal Kids

The advertisers using this technique show that the families or kids using their product are happy-go-lucky families. The ad always has a neat and well-furnished home, well-mannered kids and the family is a simple and sweet kind of family. E.g., a Dettol soap ad shows everyone in the family using that soap so is always protected from germs. They show a florescent colour line covering the whole body of each family member when compared to other people who don't use this soap.

Patriotic Advertisements

These ads show how one can support their country while he use their product or service. For example, g some products together formed a union and claimed in their ad that if you buy any one of these products, you are going to help a child to go to school. One more cellular company ad had a celebrity showing that if the customers use this company's sim card, then they can help control the population of the country.

Questioning the Customers

The advertisers using this technique ask questions to the consumers to get responses for their products. E.g., the Amway advertisement keeps on asking questions like who has so many farms completely organic in nature, who gives the strength to climb up the stairs at the age of 70, who makes the kids grow in a proper and nutritious ways, is there anyone who is listening to these entire questions. And then at last the answer comes - "Amway: We are Listening."

Bribe

This technique is used to bribe the customers with something extra if they buy the product using lines like "buy one shirt and get one free", or "be the member of the club for two years and get 20% off on all services."

Surrogate Advertising

This technique is generally used by companies which cannot advertise their products directly. The advertisers use indirect advertisements to advertise their product so that the customers know about the actual product. The biggest example of this technique is liquor ads. These ads never show anyone drinking actual liquor and in place of that they are shown drinking some mineral water, soft drink or soda.

These are the major techniques used by the advertisers to advertise their product. There are some different techniques used for online advertising such as web banner advertising in which a banner is placed on web pages, content advertising using content to advertise the product online, link advertising giving links on different sites to directly visit the product websites or advertisers.

www.ingramcontent.com/pod-product-compliance
Lightning Source LLC
Chambersburg PA
CBHW071452220526
45472CB00003B/767